Advance Praise

Find out how to mentor your next generation to become great financial stewards with this important book on wealth for families. Parents who want to instill a legacy of values, ethics, and money skills will find answers for how to engage their children, draw their family in closer, and communicate the vision they have for the future. If you're worried whether your spouse and/or adult children are prepared to manage an inheritance, there is a blueprint laid out in the pages of *Project Family Wealth*.

—Dan Sullivan
Co-Founder and President of Strategic Coach®

I've known Michelle and her family's legacy of financial wisdom for years. Her dedication to personalizing wisdom in an understandable way sets her apart from other advisors. In *Project Family Wealth*, you'll find real-world strategies that are not simply helpful for good finances but wise for life. Her emphasis on good communication with the kids—both in childhood and adulthood—is solid guidance for wealth and happiness.

—Mark Davis
Talk Show Host, 660 AM *The Answer*,
Salem Media Group, Dallas

A voice of influence and wisdom, Michelle is one of the most innovative, impassioned, empathetic, and compassionate leaders I have been fortunate to know and collaborate with for over two decades. She is a true visionary! Her holistic approach to wealth planning is unique. She redefines the integrative dimensions of family wealth: purpose and value-driven intention, generational communication, and fulfillment of lasting family legacies. *Project Family Wealth* is a 'must read'—both thought-provoking and informative. She brings a renewed approach to comprehensive family wealth planning.

—Leslee Hatch
Regional VP Delaware Life,
Certified Holistic Health Coach, CHHC

Michelle cares deeply about helping families achieve their vision of financial success. She has a unique ability to ask questions that help individuals think about scenarios for which they may need to plan way before they have occurred, giving you that "ah-ha" moment that makes you say, "Thank goodness I have Michelle looking out for me."

She goes above and beyond what you might think of as a typical "financial advisor." She's more like a financial guardian who understands your fears, anxieties, dreams, and goals and translates all of that into a living financial and investment plan that gives you confidence and peace of mind. This book shares her approach and gives insight into how to think about and manage wealth in a healthy way. Managing family wealth for over three decades, she knows what it takes to create long-lasting inheritances.

Michelle believes when families show gratitude for what they have, it creates lasting wealth. This book will change the way you approach family wealth with concepts such as identifying your *why* behind financial objectives, creating a generational mindset, and expanding the definition of wealth to include family values, traditions, and beliefs. If you are going to read a book about managing your money, this is the one!

—Susan Theder
Chief Marketing and Experience Officer, FMG

We all want the next generation to be good stewards of their money. Michelle offers keen insights into what it takes to make family wealth a successful endeavor. She creates an entire ecosystem for the care and teaching of the next generation. *Project Family Wealth* provides strategies for parents to create meaningful connections to family wealth for their heirs. She's done a terrific job giving the reader a new way to view what legacies can include. By redefining wealth to encompass family, values, virtues, life lessons, and ancestral stories, Michelle shows us we have so much more to share with the next generation.

—Bill Cawley
Chairman/CEO, Cawley Partners

The persons providing endorsements are not clients and were provided no compensation for their endorsement.

Project Family Wealth™

From the creator of
The Financial Life Map™

Project Family Wealth™

THE BLUEPRINT FOR ELIMINATING WORRY,
CLARIFYING YOUR FINANCIAL PURPOSE,
AND CREATING A LONG-LASTING INHERITANCE

MICHELLE BRENNAN HALL, CAP™

ethos
collective

Printed in the United States of America

Published by Ethos Collective™
PO Box 43, Powell, OH 43065
www.ethoscollective.vip

LCCN: 2024904157
Paperback ISBN: 978-1-63680-265-7
Hardcover ISBN: 978-1-63680-266-4
e-book ISBN: 978-1-63680-267-1

Available in paperback, hardcover, e-book, and audiobook

For my husband, Jeff, whose life journey I'm blessed to share

*To my examples of unconditional love, my sons Cameron
and Peyton, whose gracious love molds me*

*For the early lessons in courage from my parents,
Sandy & Dave Brennan, Sr.*

*And for a Heavenly Father's love that created this book
through me to write for you*

Table of Contents

Foreword

Motivational Inheritance

As a young child growing up in New Jersey, I was fortunate enough to be born into a family of Italian immigrants. My mother, father, and the rest of my family showed me the power of love, family, hard work, and dedication to grow. I am certain there is no greater motivation in life than to succeed for the benefit of yourself, but more importantly, your family and the people who are your legacy.

I look back on my childhood and realize I am fortunate to inherit my parents' values. I clearly remember their hard work in blue-collar jobs to succeed in raising a family that wanted for nothing. They defined family as those immediate (my siblings and our grandparents) but also extended to aunts, uncles, and cousins with each having a significant role in forging our family experience. They measured success based on love, impact on society, and lastly, wealth.

As I now have a family of my own and have eclipsed my parents' ability to earn wealth, I often ponder the definition of success. I have come to realize that it is the transfer of not just monetary value but wisdom, love, and mentorship to the next generation so they can succeed to greater new heights.

Soon, the next generation will take my place, and it is my hope that the transfer of this "wealth" of knowledge and dedication will enable the next generation to succeed in every way. While I relish my days as a young man working at a gas station, waiting on tables, delivering newspapers, or working with my father digging ditches, I realize that was the foundation that helped me to be successful. I understand that it's not just about money but about the ability to have enough wealth to have success in life and leave an impact on the world.

As you spend time reading this blueprint for inheritance, I think you will find that Michelle outlines the path to prepare heirs for inheriting not just money but also to guide them in being good stewards of financial assets and family values.

Perhaps the best way to understand the power of inheritance is to realize that money can be a vehicle to not only provide material goods but also opportunity. If you take the time to nurture the wealth that you have, it will provide an opportunity for everything else you'd like to accomplish in life leaving a legacy for generations to build on.

After being in financial services for more than thirty-two years and being fortunate to manage billions of dollars for thousands of families, I know the individuals remembered best are those who took the time to engage, mentor, and plan for his/her heirs. While I can assure you that investing is part of the success, planning for the outcome, as well as engaging your family can build a blueprint for generations.

Philip S. Blancato
Chief Market Strategist, Advisor Group
President & CEO, Ladenburg Thalmann Asset Management

The Meaning of the Open Ensō

The image on this book's cover, the open ensō circle, is a Japanese symbol that represents the circle of togetherness.

It is traditionally drawn with one singularly uninterrupted brushstroke without any modification afterward. Chances are you're already familiar with the ensō circle—even if you don't know its name—because it's been incorporated into many logos in business, technology, and even finance.

When the circle is closed, it represents perfection. When the circle is open, it represents perfection yet to be achieved. The meaning is that as one undertakes any effort, it is done so with the mindset of enjoying the journey ahead.

You've accumulated financial assets and may have done some financial planning already, but there's work yet to be done. This journey—or project—is the purpose of the book: managing family wealth, passing on gifts of our life's stories, handing the baton to the next generation, educating the next generation on how to be financially independent, and creating family traditions that stand the test of time over generations. It's not an effort in perfection but an effort in love.

This blueprint for long-lasting inheritances is my way of imparting how successful families have infused love into their efforts to plan their estates and impact generations. To do so is an ongoing effort that isn't a race for short-lived closure but for enduring familial connection.

As your family grows and uses the gifts you've shared with them, they will carry on your legacy and create legacies of their own in a never-ending cycle that impacts your family and the world around you for generations.

Visual symbols like family crests serve as powerful tools, and so does the ensō circle. Use the circle as a unifying crest for this process. Treat this simple circle as a reminder of what you're hoping to achieve for yourself and your family. Take advantage of this chance in time to create a lasting legacy that serves as a blueprint for future generations.

Imagine your life's impact continuing on through many generations. Imagine what values you can impart and the stories of your life's work being told generation after generation. **Imagine the impact.**

Planning for the future takes work, but I hope you also enjoy the many moments of family togetherness that occur during this journey. When you step into this work with a future-focused mindset, you'll be able to create a Project Family Wealth of your own—a gift that strives to meet the needs of your family during this lifetime and also provides future generations with knowledge, connection, and assets to cycle your legacy forward, one brushstroke at a time.

Introduction

Getting the Most Out of Project Family Wealth

You are one decision away from a completely different life.

—Mel Robbins

Family, for many of us, is at the root of our most meaningful goals and motivations. A family is defined by the members who have come before and the individuals who are alive today, and it continues to be shaped by future descendants. That's why each family has dreams for the future and aspirations for generations to come.

As a key member of your family, now is your time to influence your family's legacy and safeguard future generations.

We only have this one life, so we should take advantage of the time given to us. Yet planning for the future is easier said than done. It's complicated, and there's so much to do that it can be hard to know where to start. So what do you do?

Typically, you meet with an estate attorney and have them draft estate documents for your spouse and heirs to direct assets. You invest, each year, toward a retirement date plucked out of thin air. You get life insurance. And you hope that it will be enough to carry you and your spouse through retirement with something left over for the kids to inherit. You do all this because it's the right thing to do.

But is it really? Is there something more to financial and estate planning that is missing from the typical approach? I believe so.

The truth is that the standard estate-planning checklist doesn't cut it anymore. It only deals with money and assets, but setting up your family for long-term financial resilience is about more than assets. Do you have more than money to pass on? Could there be more in what you've accumulated in life that your heirs would cherish? Are your children prepared to inherit the wealth you've worked your whole life to earn?

If you're like many of my clients when they first step into my office, you've never been asked these questions before. Most investors follow a financial checklist without much thought as to why their goals hold importance. You may have defined objectives and established a plan to achieve them as you should, but have you ever pondered the *why* behind your life intentions?

If you haven't, now is the time to find your answers.

Bringing My Insight to Your Family

Before we begin, I want to introduce myself as your guide in planning your family's financial future. How can my expertise help you achieve your goals?

I am afforded the great blessing of three decades of guiding family wealth. Today, as founder and wealth advisor at Brennan Wealth Advisors, I help clients in my home state of Texas and throughout the country find clarity about the road ahead as they manage the many aspects of family wealth.

However, investing is usually only 25 percent of how I interact with clients. The rest of my role involves what I call "the other side of money." Encouraging spousal engagement, mentoring inheritors, expanding the concept of wealth to include family values, and advising families on how to handle wealth in a collaborative and caring way.

As a wealth advisor, I want to make sure my clients, their spouses, children, grandchildren, and the generations beyond are considered and cared for in the estate-planning process so they can lead meaningful lives and be financially resilient long into the future. This ambition is what we all want for our family, isn't it?

I come from a family of financial advisors, and over the years, I've learned about financial resilience both professionally and personally. My parents grew up in low-income households, but they worked hard, loved their families, and wanted more out of life. They met at work and were determined to do all they could to make a better life for the family they dreamed of having. This process started with smart money habits and thoughtful savings.

Each pay period, they set aside cash in envelopes labeled rent, food, gas, and college. My mom's salary paid for my dad to go to night school to get his degree, and gradually, they worked their plan toward significance—not for themselves, but to influence the four children they would eventually have.

Believing in a strong work ethic, education, and America as the land of opportunity for dreamers, my parents raised my siblings and me with the motto, "You can be anything you want to be."

I believed it. Still do.

That motto was the thread that wove through my childhood and made me the person I am today. While raising two sons with my husband, we knew how important a family motto could be. Our boys grew up hearing, "You are the only you the entire world has, so be sure to take care of the vessel."

I imagine you may have a motto you would like to communicate to your family but never found the right opportunity. By reading this book, it is my intention that you will have a framework to create a family team effort to be on the same page about money, values, and your vision for the future.

Who Should Read This Book?

Throughout my career, I've had the privilege of managing wealth for high-net-worth individuals and families of all shapes and sizes. That said, more often than not, my clients fit a particular pattern.

They are typically male and the major financial provider for the family. He is the financial decision-maker, and his spouse tends to be uninvolved in managing family finances. He cares deeply about the well-being of his loved ones, and he's concerned about his family's ability to remain fiscally resilient in the future after he's gone. He worries about what his wife will do when he is gone and fears that an inheritance he leaves to his children could be mismanaged instead of serving as a catalyst to improve their lives.

For simplicity's sake, I've phrased many messages throughout the book to speak to this audience. However, make no mistake: if you play a role in managing your family's wealth, regardless of your gender, marital status, or number of children, this book is for you.

Your Guide to Family Wealth

I wrote this book to empower families to reach their destinies. After all, you know you are meant for more, and so is your family.

As you turn each page, I encourage you to think about the thread that will weave your family together. Creating lasting change may sound idyllic, but what if your intention could lead your entire family to pursue the destinies they're meant for? What if it could inspire them to live incredible lives? And what if a newly imagined perspective on family wealth could help them achieve their goals rather than cause family conflict?

Your family's generational wealth is one of your life's greatest works, and you're the leader of that project. The family CEO. The difference between success and struggles within your family may come down to your actions.

I've seen exceptional families succeed in creating, caring for, and transferring wealth in all its facets. These are families with courageous leadership. They openly discuss money decisions, encourage each other to develop financial skills, and teach the younger generations how to be fiscally prudent. But most importantly, they lead with the question, "Why?"

Asking *why* is at the heart of all inspiration. Furthermore, these successful families develop a chain of command for financial decision-making that recognizes everyone's strengths.

For each successful family I encounter, I also witness many more families who struggle to protect and plan for the transfer of wealth. These are the families that devolve into conflict when the primary decision-maker is no longer around. Often, the spouse—usually the matriarch—has not been involved in the financial planning process and becomes overwhelmed when suddenly thrust into the family's leadership role.

The biggest culprit that wreaks havoc in families is a lack of communication. Unfortunately, many families avoid the topic of money completely and treat it as a taboo topic. We've gotten to the point where talking to your kids about sex is more socially accepted than talking to your kids about money. Others discuss wealth and come together around shared values to successfully shape their family's future.

Both sets of families—the families that successfully transfer wealth and the ones that struggle—offer valuable lessons. One of the most important lessons is this word of warning: money can do bad things to good people, so be sure to handle it with care. Without proper leadership and an overtly discussed wealth plan, family members will be left to figure out the details on their own, which is where most problems begin.

For many parents, their biggest fear is that their children may squander an inheritance. Most parents didn't work their entire lives so their kids could buy ski boats, lake houses, or flashy cars—they want the money to go toward something more meaningful.

When heirs develop poor money habits, their behavior tends to become a point of contention for family members. Judgment occurs, and this introduces conflict and turmoil within the family. If the next generation does not learn how to manage wealth, long-lasting inheritances may not be achievable.

Sadly, this fallout occurs more often than not. Consider these startling inheritance facts:

- According to a 2015 article by Elizabeth O'Brien of Market Watch, based on Federal Reserve data, one-third of inheritors have negative savings two years after inheriting money.[1]
- In a study on wealthy families, The Williams Group found that 70 percent of family wealth is gone by the second generation; by the third generation, 90 percent is gone.[2]

Imagine spending decades accumulating wealth, only for it to be spent within a few short years. You undoubtedly don't want this to happen in your family. Fortunately, you can take steps to prevent this outcome starting right now.

Lead Your Family with Intention

Protecting your family from the negative influences of wealth means being intentional about how your assets transfer to

---

[1]   Elizabeth O'Brien, "One in Three Americans Who Get an Inheritance Blow It - Marketwatch," MarketWatch, September 3, 2015, https:// www.marketwatch.com/story/one-in-three-americans-who-get-an-inheritance-blow-it-2015-09-03.

[2]   Jeff Wuorio, "How to Avoid Being the 70 Percent Who Squander Their Inheritance," Deseret News, September 4, 2016, https:// www.deseret.com/2016/9/4/20595426/how-to-avoid-being-the-70-percent-who-squander-their-inheritance/#:~:text=Take%20 steps%20to%20preserve%20as,avoid%20having%20to%20 probate%20assets.

your heirs. It takes starting conversations about money with your spouse and children. Above all, it takes teaching your children about the true value of money, your dreams for the family, and your hopes for them.

These lessons will be grounded in your intentions for your family's future. Better yet, I'm giving you my tools to make that future a reality. But if you're expecting a typical book on wealth that includes graphs, charts, and stock strategies, this book will be different from all of that.

This book is not your typical investing book—there are enough of those already. Rather, this is a book about the non-money conversations that need to happen around wealth. It contains lessons designed to inspire you to lead your family members to be financially resilient. It's the beginning of an ongoing process—a new tradition and a new way of managing your family, not a one-and-done exercise.

Maybe you've tried talking about money and values with your family, only for your discussions not to go as planned. That's a common problem. Discussions about money can be awkward. Your children may seem like they don't care about money, or it might be uncomfortable to discuss. But the subjects around wealth, values, traditions, and goals are important to address with your family. Furthermore, while it may seem like your children are uninterested in money itself, I can assure you that they're interested in hearing the story behind the money. *Your* life story.

The good news is that it's never too late to begin this project with your loved ones. Your children likely value a connection with you as much as you do with them. As you contemplate your gifts and the *why* behind your goals, I offer this question to begin the process: **"In ten years, you will be ten years older. Why not train the people you love most to be able to receive the baton when you pass it to them?"**

Getting the Most Out of *Project Family Wealth*

As you dive into this book, I'd like to give you some tips on how to extract the most value from its pages. You'll notice **some phrases are highlighted in bold font.** These are key ideas worth a little extra attention. If you take away nothing else from this book, take the bolded concepts.

You'll also see information in pop-out boxes like this one. These boxes contain auxiliary information that can help deepen your understanding of the main text.

I've included actionable steps throughout the book that can guide you in putting *Project Family Wealth* into motion right away in your own family. Action drives results, so I encourage you to give these activities a try.

Lastly, each chapter ends with a summary of its key concepts. If you want to revisit an earlier chapter, refresh your memory, or even prime yourself before reading a chapter, the summary is a great place to start.

I believe you have a powerful moment in time to significantly influence your family. That time is now. There is no richer time in life than now. Let's use it well so you can *live* well.

This is why I wrote the book.

I want you to enjoy your time with your family now, share your values and stories with them, and lead your family to long-term financial success. So many investors plan for a single time in the future, but in doing so, they miss the chance to enjoy the journey.

As you read this book, I hope you're reminded to enjoy the journey every time you see the Open Ensō. Remember that the journey is now, and your loved ones would benefit greatly from a coordinated focus on what wealth really means in your family.

The most important skill we can hone in life is to be a leader—a good one—and to mentor others to be leaders as well.

If you're not already engaging with your family on the subject of wealth and values, it's never too late to start. Now is that time—we can always change. I've seen it happen many times in the lives of my clients, and it's so rewarding to watch a family transform. It takes only a spark, a thought, a book, maybe.

In the coming chapters, I hope to broaden your definition of wealth, challenge your thoughts about who *really* owns your legacy, and offer a blueprint to care for your spouse and heirs both while you are here and when you are gone.

So let's get started.

1

What Is at the Heart of Your Why?

Let us all be the leaders we wish we had.

—Simon Sinek

In Simon Sinek's famous TED Talk, he shares a concept called the Golden Circle. Inside the circle is why we do what we do. He posits that good leaders talk about *what* and *how* they do what they do, but exceptional leaders speak about *why* they do what they do and *why* they operate that way. This is a concept worth exploring in life as you think about your family's present and future.

Goals for yourself, your children, and your family's future generations all connect deeply with your personal *why*. What is your *why*?

> **Your *why* is the reason you do what you do. It's the source of your motivation—the force that drives you to get out of bed every morning. It's why you got married and had children, and it's the reason you work hard and have financial goals. It is your ultimate aspiration.**

Your *why* also encompasses the values you hold. For example, maybe you value the experience gained from trade schools or the freedom of self-employment. Perhaps making charitable contributions is important, or you value a frugal way of life, or you're driven to mentor and educate the next generation. It's how you raise your family, why you have the beliefs you have, and what motivates your thoughts.

We sometimes forget to share our *why* and the purpose of our actions with others. But imagine for a moment a discussion with your wife where you tell her she is the reason you work hard, started a company, and continue to provide the life you have together. That she is the heart of your *why*.

Whatever it is that you value, sharing your motivations with your family will create a powerful connection. In doing so, your family sees the act of having values and the *why* attached to them, which makes goal achievement meaningful. It gives each family member the opportunity to develop their view of the world and to see how they fit into the fabric of the family.

What Do Your Goals Represent?

As you can see, this chapter is about defining yourself as a person, a parent, a spouse, and an investor because when you get clarity on your motivation, you can help connect family to the purpose of why to invest and save for the future and how important it is to create long-lasting inheritances. This is a powerful driver when it comes to family wealth.

To define your *why*, start by asking yourself the question, "Why do I have financial goals?"

Many possible reasons exist: you want to get ahead, prepare for the future, buy a home, send your kids or grandchildren to college, purchase a lake or mountain house, donate to charity, start a new business, or create a longevity plan for a long, active retirement.

Let's say you have financial goals for several of these reasons. The real reason you have these goals goes beyond "because it's what you're supposed to do." The heart of your *why* is more about what your goals represent. *Why* does it matter if your kids go to college? *Why* do you want to support charitable causes? *Why* is it important to invest in a longevity plan for retirement?

The client families I work with who take this concept to heart work diligently to translate their *why* to heirs. In the end, they transform into the most successful families in the matter of creating long-lasting inheritances.

Consider the following *why*s behind some common financial goals:

- **"I want to save enough money to make sure my wife is taken care of."** In this case, the *why* is that the spouse wants to prepare his wife for when he is gone. He loves her and wants to be sure she'll be okay financially on her own. Her peace of mind will give him peace of mind.

- **"I don't want to be a burden to my family in retirement."** In other words, this couple doesn't want their kids to suffer financially if they need health care in the future, so it's important for them to save now. Financial independence in retirement is key.
- **"We want to pay for college education."** Parents often say this because they don't want their children to enter adulthood with financial debt when they graduate. They want to give their children the best possible chance at a good education and successful life.
- **"When I'm gone, I want a charity to receive half of my estate."** This person's *why* is to make a significant impact in their community and improve the lives of those around them. They also want to be remembered as benevolent and charitable.

Each of the examples above has an underlying reason or *why* that motivates the goal. In answering the question, "What is *your why?*" make sure to dig deep and get at the heart of your real motivations.

Share Your Why Through Family Stories

Don't underestimate the value of family stories. They are a powerful way to weave a thread from generation to generation by telling tales of family hardships, heroism, risks taken, and life-changing decisions.

Sharing stories of other generations is a perfect way to bring meaning to holiday dinners and time together. It's so important for children to be linked to family lineage and to understand why they themselves are in this family and how meaningful they are to the future.

Decide what you want to preserve and pass down, and in the coming chapters, we'll explore approaches for how you can do exactly that. This begins the process not only of connecting the family but also of helping each family member connect to their *why*.

Consider a Texan client of mine. In Texas, family ranches are a *big* deal. For many people, inheriting a ranch is practically a rite of passage, and they're taught to value the family's land from the time they're children. This client of mine had inherited his family's ranch and was now in his late seventies when the state offered to buy his acreage for a new development. They planned to construct a major thoroughfare across his land through what had once been nothing but cattle and tumbleweeds.

My client, however, refused to sell all of his property. He told me, "I will never sell all of the acreage because I, too, will be buried on my family's land."

This was a man who knew what he valued and had acted with intention to preserve it. His family had lived on that land for generations. They'd cared for the property and the animals, and being a part of that family legacy was important to him—more important than any money the state could offer.

When my client shared stories about the family ranch with his children, his *why* clicked for them. They understood the reasons their father wanted to preserve that land and keep it in the family. When the children were able to connect the ranch to meaningful family stories, it became more than just an asset to them, and their personal *whys* expanded to include a respect and appreciation for the family land.

I encourage you to think about what generational wealth could look like for your family. Three generations from now, what family values, traditions, and assets would you want your descendants to cherish? What stories from your life would you want them to know?

The reality is that you never stop being a parent. Whether it's intentional or not, we as parents are giving our children messages their entire lifetimes: monetary lessons, values, experiences, and purpose. Your children will continue learning from you long after they reach adulthood, so it's important to live with intention and connect with your values.

What Is the Value of an Apprenticeship?

As you launch Project Family Wealth, you can think of your family as your team members. Your spouse is your business partner, and your children are your apprentices. But before we move ahead with this analogy, you might be wondering, "Why do my children need an 'apprenticeship' in the matters of wealth?"

The answer is simple: so they'll be prepared to handle their financial future independently as well as manage an inheritance.

Teach your children about family wealth and connect them to your *why* and to each other. Prepare them and take them under your wing—a wealth apprenticeship, if you will. When family leaders let inheritances be a surprise instead, the results can be disastrous.

To demonstrate how things can go wrong when inheritances are a surprise, consider the following example of a man who ran a successful family business. He managed sales for the company while his wife handled the office administration.

This couple had two sons and a daughter, and at a certain point, they brought in one of their sons and their son-in-law to work for the company. The son-in-law was much more astute in business than the son; he was the logical choice for a successor. However, the parents didn't establish a chain of command for the next generation of leadership. Even though the patriarch was approaching his seventies, it was hard for him to think of himself as anything but immortal.

This father also struggled with the decision to appoint his son-in-law to a higher position than his own son. "How could I do that to him?" he'd ask.

He put off the decision until, unfortunately, he developed dementia. At that point, it was too late to plan, and the wife and adult children were left to figure out the management and future of the business on their own. They didn't know how to access all the business accounts, pay the necessary bills, or stay in touch with the company's top clients. Ultimately, this chaos tore the family apart.

If the patriarch in the story above had taken the step to appoint his son-in-law as the next head of the company and explained what needed to happen next and why, his family would have been in a much better position. They could have avoided many sleepless nights.

> The reality is that successful financial planning requires a mind shift. It takes strong leadership to make the right decisions for your family's financial future. Sometimes, the decisions aren't easy, but it's important to do what's best for your family.

In contrast to the story above, consider a different family that made the effort to prepare their children to manage wealth. This family included a matriarch and patriarch who were extremely charitable. Every year, they donated to nearly thirty different charities, and when their children were old enough to be involved, the parents brought them into the process.

It was important to these parents that they could donate together with their children in an extensive and purposeful way. To do that, they established a foundation and charitable trust that the whole family was involved in managing. The parents were able to enjoy the life-changing experience of seeing how thoughtful their adult children had grown up to be. They valued the perspectives their children brought to the table, and overall, the shared mission solidified what they stood for as a family. Even though each member of the family had a different personality and viewpoint, they were able to work together toward a shared goal.

This beautiful outcome and evolution would not have happened if the parents hadn't informed and educated their children about the family's charitable giving. The most poignant part of the story is that the parents welcomed the family into the charitable experience with them. That's why it's so important to bring adult children into the discussion about family wealth early. **Once you've made financial decisions with your spouse, share them with your kids.**

Manage Wealth with Purpose and Intention

At this point, you might be thinking that it takes a great deal of mental work to discover your *why* and communicate it to your family. My advice is to not make this endeavor bigger than it has to be. This work is worth the effort, but it doesn't need to be onerous. Remember that you're laying the groundwork for your family's legacy, hopefully for generations to come.

True, you could do none of this work. You could follow the standard financial- and estate-planning checklist, let your heirs spend their inheritance as they please, and hope for the best. But what a lost opportunity! We get only one shot at this life, so why not be intentional about how you raise your family around money and purposeful in how you use your wealth?

Remember, you have a powerful moment in time to impact your family's destiny.

Equally crucial is that you communicate these decisions—and the reasoning behind them—to your family members so you can move forward together. Successful families live intentionally and transparently. They understand that for the next generation to be successful at inheriting, they need to be taught how to be responsible with money. This requires heirs to be connected to the family's

Intention is a major differentiator between families who succeed at creating long-lasting inheritances and those who do not. Leaders in successful families know that being intentional is at the center of their financial future.

financial wealth, not for money's sake, but through stories, values, and the *why* behind the money. In other words, they're connected for respect's sake.

Work Together as a Team

In your role as the head of the family, you're leading family members to come together as a team to work on Project Family Wealth.

Your children, and perhaps even your grandchildren, are your apprentices. Your spouse is the co-manager of this project, and your kids need to see her engaged in the process for there to be participation from everybody.

Each person naturally has their own goals in life, but you can still share a vision for the family's future. A reminder: if your spouse is already fully engaged in family financial plans, terrific! But in my experience with my clients, ninety-five percent of the time, that isn't the case.

Furthermore, just as though you were executing a business project, it's necessary to consider your resources and the team members who will be involved. Recognize that each person brings unique skills to the table. Adding more perspectives to your endeavor is a strength, and as the family's leader, you can make sure to apply those skills in the right areas.

Success depends upon communicating a vision to your family members so everyone can move in the same direction—toward financial resilience and generational wealth.

Actionable Steps

Step #1: Find Your *Why* in Values

As you explore your *why*, it's useful to identify the values you find important in life. Values tend to inform your *why*, so you can't have one without the other.

Below is a list of values, skills, and principles to consider. Some may resonate with you.

Select twelve values that are most important to you.

Once you have twelve selected, **narrow your list down to six**.

From there, **identify the three values that you cannot imagine living without**.

Adaptability	Faithfulness	Knowledge	Reputation
Adventure	Family	Leadership	Respect
Ambition	Freedom	Loyalty	Responsibility
Autonomy	Friendship	Open-mindedness	Security
Charity	Frugality	Optimism	Selflessness
Commitment	Generosity	Order	Self-expression
Community	Growth	Patience	Self-reliance
Diplomacy	Hardworking	Peace of mind	Serenity
Diversity	Honesty	Personal Growth	Sincerity
Economic security	Humility	Pleasure	Sophistication
Education	Individuality	Prestige	Spirituality
Empowerment	Influence	Privacy	Stability
Ethics	Innovation	Purity	Travel
Excellence	Integrity	Purpose	Visionary
Expertise	Justice	Relationships	Wisdom
Fairness	Kindness	Religion	Wit

Values Exercise

List your 12 most important Values from the list above:

_____	_____	_____
_____	_____	_____
_____	_____	_____
_____	_____	_____

Narrow your list of 12 Values down to 6 Values:

_____	_____	_____
_____	_____	_____

From your list of 6 Values above, select the Top Three Values that best describe you:

_____	_____	_____

Step #2: Make It a Family Activity

Once you've completed the values exercise, ask your spouse, your children, and even your grandchildren to do the same. Have everyone choose their values so you can all compare and discuss your answers. You might be surprised how receptive your loved ones can be.

For example, one family I coached in this manner said they saw a ripple effect take place when they intentionally spoke to their kids about drivers, meaning, and the future. In other words, the parents took the first step in starting the conversation, but the positive effect of the discussion was amplified by the children. Drivers are what get us in motion to live out our values. For example, if I value philanthropy, a driver may be serving on a non-profit board. Meaning is then derived from the contribution of time and talent. This then leads us to an ever-expanding future.

These parents chose to communicate in their own words, which resonated with their teenage kids. Filled with deep, meaningful emotion, the children felt inspired to be a part of the family's focus—their *why*.

Imagine having a talk with your kids about money, wealth, and the future that ends in enthusiasm!

Remember, each of us is looking for significance, and discussions like this can be quite inspiring. All you need to do is start the conversation.

Step #3: Consider Drivers, Meaning, and Future

Now that you've identified your values, let's further define your *why* by answering the following questions:

Drivers: What inspires your wealth objectives?

_____

_____

_____

_____

Meaning: Why are these inspirations important?

_____

_____

_____

_____

Future: What do you want to teach and pass on to the children in your life while you are here?

_____

_____

_____

_____

Future: What could your family stand for?

_____

_____

_____

_____

Step #4: "So That" Exercise

When I first meet with clients, I listen intently to discover the *why* behind their objectives. Of course, no one usually outright says, "This is my *why* behind my wealth goals," so I've learned to read between the lines and ask probing questions. I listen for keywords that clue me in to their motivations: "so that," "because," and "in order to…."

Most people have many goals, but there's usually a single strong motivating factor that powers each family member's decisions. Knowing this *why* is the difference between setting a goal and achieving a goal.

The purpose of this exercise is to gain insight into your family members' *whys*. When you're going through this process and discussing your *why* with your family, listen for these "so that" statements from them.

Consider these prompts to help you and your family articulate the heart of your *whys*:

What traditions could lead our family to _____ so that _____?

What stories of my parents' lives would be important to share so that _____?

How can I teach my children the power of independence so that _____?

Thinking about ten years from now, what impact in the community would I want to work on with my family because _____?

How can my spouse and I act intentionally with our financial values so that we inspire _____ in our children and grandchildren?

What ideas were bestowed upon me early in life that are important to pass down for generations so that _____?

The answers to the questions above can help bring each person's *why* into the light so you can better understand and connect with one another.

The steps above don't require much time, but they go a long way toward forging stronger family connections and getting you, your spouse, and your children on the same page about your *whys*.

Key Concepts

- You have a powerful moment in time to prepare your family for a lifetime of financial resilience. As the leader of Project Family Wealth in your household, it's up to you to establish an open and honest dialogue with your spouse and children so you can effectively pass on your values, stories, lessons, and goals—the necessary ingredients for long-lasting inheritances.

- Your first step in Project Family Wealth is to define your *why*—the motivation behind your financial goals.

- To determine your *why*, think about what you want out of life. Also, consider the values you've taught your children. Both can bring clarity to the things that matter most to you.

- Next, encourage your children to identify the *why* of their goals.

- As you embark on Project Family Wealth, think of your children as your apprentices. You likely have more to teach them than you realize, and we'll explore approaches for how you can transfer wealth in all its aspects in the following chapters.

- Being intentional in your financial decisions is a major differentiator between families who succeed in preserving family wealth and those who struggle.

2

The Pillars of Wealth™

Wealth is the ability to fully experience life.
—Henry David Thoreau

Many people picture wealth accumulation as the only inheritance asset that matters. They ignore all the other gifts they are able to give that can inspire family or impact the community. However, since you're reading this book, we both know that the opposite describes you.

You care deeply about your family and want to preserve traditions and encourage mindsets that are passed on to help later generations thrive. You care about your *why*, but you might not know how to start these conversations. I've developed a framework for families to create an action plan using an easy tool: the Pillars of Wealth.

Traditionally, we think about inheritance in terms of physical assets—houses, cars, investments, and bank accounts—but wealth can also be intangible and take the form of knowledge, life experiences, traditions, heritage, and time together that you pass on.

Your Legacy Is More Than Assets

The Pillars of Wealth is a conceptual way to think about the legacy gifts you create over a lifetime. After all, your legacy is a lot more than just passing on money and other assets.

When we are gone, we want to be remembered for much more than the assets of our estate. Memories, traditions, values, and stories that live on through family make a life well-lived so much richer. As the head of your family, I'm sure you want to inspire your children and grandchildren to strive for beautiful, fulfilled lives and accomplishments beyond what they can imagine.

This book is about leaving behind as much of yourself as possible. Thinking about inheritance from this perspective broadens the concept of wealth and creates the opportunity for long-lasting connections with family.

Now that you've spent some time thinking about what is at the heart of your *why* when it comes to money matters, it's time to zoom out and look at a framework for Project Family Wealth.

When I work with families, we use the Pillars of Wealth to identify their areas of strength and the areas they want to enhance. Each family is unique in this aspect.

The illustration below shows how the heart of your *why* is central to the interaction of each of the quadrants. You could say it is the vision and mission of why you do what you do.

Pillars of Wealth

EXPERIENCE
- **Traditions**
- **Perspectives**
- **Inspiring Heirs**

LEGACY LEARNING
- **Generational Engagement**
- **The Story Behind the Money**
- **Heritage**

HEART OF THE WHY

ASSETS
- **Financial**
- **Intentional Values**
- **Power of Independence**

PURPOSE
- **Impact**
- **Gifting**
- **Leadership**

Families that are in touch with all four pillars think about their assets, traditions, and values, how they inspire heirs, and how to tell the stories of family ancestry. This is the process that begins linking heirs to the true meaning of inheritance.

By using the four pillars as a framework to talk about wealth, you can inspire your family to work together. Think of it as having the right scaffolding to support, build, and create your family's intentions toward financial resiliency. With this perspective on wealth, now is the time to ask yourself and your family members, "What do I really want in the future?"

For instance, you may want a lake house as a place to create family traditions. Is there an annual family trip you can create to share family lineage and heritage stories of your family business or ranch? Or maybe you want the next generation to build an addition to the local children's hospital. It may be important for your grandchildren to see other cultures on annual exploration trips. Could you schedule family meetings to engage and educate family members in long-term family planning?

Viewing wealth in this manner links meaning to the assets. This is what most estate plans leave out. It is also why most families fail at working cohesively when inheritances are passed down. The meaning is missing. The stories go untold. The traditions never started. Purpose is absent. When people are only connected to money for money's sake, the opportunity for long-lasting inheritances can be lost.

The pillars ensure that you and your family broaden your view of wealth.

So why this larger vision of wealth? If all we teach the next generation about our lives is that it was a pursuit of accumulating assets, we will truly leave them very little, no matter the amount of inheritance.

Wealth consists of all that we can give from our life experiences: love and wisdom, time and support, financial assets and values, stories of triumph, and even tales of life's challenges. These are the Pillars of Wealth that become the legacy your heirs amplify and carry on.

Everyone comes to the financial planning table thinking about money, but I encourage you to go beyond the face value of inheritance. Dig deeper. Create a connection between your heirs and the purpose of their inheritance. Your children and grandchildren will thank you for it.

Understanding Wealth in All Its Aspects

Now that you've been introduced to the Pillars of Wealth, let's explore how wealth is defined in each category. My goal is to expand the traditional definition of wealth so investors understand there is much more to give than financial assets. As a result, heirs stand to gain a much more meaningful inheritance than just money. This perspective will also be helpful as you prepare to pass the baton to the next generation.

Assets

The Assets Pillar includes physical assets that we traditionally think of as inheritances. It also includes certain intangibles like intentions around asset accumulation and the importance of achieving financial independence. These intangibles shape your children's money habits as well as their moral compass and help put heirs on the path of long-term financial responsibility. It's about linking the how of managing money to the *why* behind financial aspirations.

Financial

Your financial assets are, perhaps, the most straightforward component of your wealth. Financial assets include anything that adds to your net worth: investments, real estate, vehicles, bank accounts, businesses, heirlooms, and valuables.

Intentional Values

Intentional values explain why you handle wealth the way you do. For example, these values inform how much you want in a savings account for peace of mind or explain why you drive your truck a hundred thousand miles before buying a new one. It is the reason you and your spouse donate 10 percent of your income each year.

If one of your values is family togetherness, you might buy a mountain house because it's a great opportunity to bring your whole family together. By sharing the *why* behind the purchase of the lake house, you guide your entire family to have their own connection to wealth as well. You help your family understand the full value behind the asset: "The lake house is more than a vacation property or real-estate investment; it's a chance for us to grow closer as a family."

If you intend to leave money to your adult children so they can lead a debt-free life, tell them. If you want your heirs to use their inheritance for retirement income, tell them. If you wish for them to carry on the family tradition of annual contributions to the family's beloved charity, tell them.

Power of Independence

Money can't buy happiness or love, but it sure does make life easier. The power of independence is just that: knowing you have the financial ability to live an incredible life without money worries. In other words, it describes the financial choices that support independence.

The power of independence is about making the right financial moves as much as it is a mindset. **A pivotal point in our lives is when we realize that our financial journey is ours alone and that being independent or dependent is our individual choice.** This could be the single most powerful gift you can pass on to your family: the knowledge that they, too, can achieve financial freedom.

Experience

The Experience Pillar concerns actions and ideas—traditions you practice, perspectives you hold, and the inspiration you provide to younger generations.

Traditions

Traditions play an important role in many families, whether they're centered around holidays, anniversaries, shared activities, or other meaningful events.

To make traditions a part of your family's generational wealth, start by identifying them. Name them. I have a dear friend and mentor, Lee Brower, whose family named their holiday gathering "Thanksmas." They practice gratitude daily and encourage finding gratitude in all of life's experiences.

Thanksmas is their time to honor that tradition and share the best gratitude moments of the year. Every year, each person traces their handprint on a white tablecloth and writes one word of gratitude and the date inside their handprint. They have great fun looking for each others' prints from year to year.

This is your opportunity to create family traditions that align with your *why*. For example, if you value helping the community, you may decide to spend every Thanksgiving serving lunch to those experiencing food insecurity. Keep in mind that traditions don't have to be grandiose—they can be as simple as deciding which household hosts Christmas dinner. (Not all traditions center around eating, but most of mine do—and you might find it's the same with your family.)

Bring the kids into these conversations by asking them what traditions they'd like to try. You might learn that they'd like to start a family game night, a Sunday dinner where everyone cooks together, or a yearly crawfish boil. Talking about traditions is a great way to have meaningful conversations with your family, and it's likely going to be more memorable than a lesson about finances.

Perspectives

Perspectives form another valuable component of wealth. Your heirs will benefit from hearing your perspective, and you'll benefit from hearing theirs. Creating a collaborative environment where everyone's unique strengths are heard is essential to a sustainable generational mindset.

As an example, my parents always loved time together as a family. They frequently hosted gatherings at their house and traveled the world to meet new people and hear different points of view. They instilled in us the importance of travel and time together, which reinforced the necessity of being open to understanding different perspectives.

My husband and I carry that forward with our sons by traveling outside the United States with them often. Our youngest son is a history buff, and our eldest son is a foodie, so we make sure to infuse tours and trips with local history and cuisine. On each trip, we plan an event or excursion that includes something we have never done before. We call it our "Courage Act." Some adventures have been exhilarating and a bit out of our comfort zone (like ziplining and a ropes course), but the experience leaves us with a lifetime of memories and stories.

Inspiring Heirs

Another piece of the Experience Pillar is the inspiration you give to your family. When you inspire your heirs, you encourage them to pursue their dreams and uphold their values. Sharing your personal stories is not only the cornerstone of inspiring the next generation but also helping them think outside of the box, teaching them to stand up for something, and showing them how to find ways to give to others. This is how we inspire the next generation.

Legacy

The Legacy Pillar concerns what comes next—your family's future—and the actions you take today that will influence tomorrow. It asks, "What will you pass on to the next generation?"

As you move forward, the pillar helps to look back at where you've come from, which is why the Legacy Pillar also includes your family's heritage. Even if you don't have personal memories of family ancestors, you can start by passing down your family story to your children and grandchildren.

Each family has a story worth telling. Some family stories are grand, while others are difficult, but what the next generation does also becomes part of the story. **Remember, our legacy is not really ours—it is in the hands of the next generation.**

This book was written in 2022. Some would describe this year and the two years prior as difficult for our nation. Many focus on the aftereffects of the 2020 pandemic: rising crime, political bickering, Russia's war on Ukraine, and rising costs due to inflation. These shocking world events happened, but they do not have to define us.

One of my clients said she worries about this generation of kids and what kind of world her grandchildren will live in. I said, "Don't worry; do something about it. Talk to your grandkids. Tell them stories of goodness and hope, your upbringing, and how you view the world. Give them something to hold on to. If you don't, someone else will."

We are all responsible for the next generation.

Generational Engagement

I'm drawn to stories about generational family businesses, not only because I can personally relate but because it is intriguing to see how a business can tie a family together. Successful family businesses require relatives who are united with purpose and respect. The key to their success is generational engagement: providing opportunities for mentorship and involvement.

The Quiring family in Canada is a fourth-generation towing company that works on one of the iciest and most treacherous highways in North America. They rescue individuals from jackknifed eighteen-wheelers, flipped cars, and pile-ups on the highway caused by freezing conditions. The members of the Quiring family receive training and mentoring in the business at an early age—sometimes as young as fifteen or sixteen years old—and use the knowledge from previous generations to help save motorists. In this way, they're a living embodiment of how generational engagement can unite a family around a shared vision.

To build generational engagement, it's important to never underestimate the power of mentorship in your family. You are the head of your family and you can be an important motivator in the life journey of your heirs. They are your apprentices, and they need and value your guidance. When we leave this Earth, we leave only our children and our reputation behind. What a gift to the world this can be.

I encourage you to use the pillars to create moments in your life that pave the way for your heirs. All we truly have is the here and now, and each day creates a pavestone opportunity on the pathway of our lives. That pathway can then be used by others as a blueprint for *their* lives: family, colleagues, people in your industry, and even those you may never know.

We each have a story to tell, so tell yours well. Pave the hell out of this life and blaze a trail for others!

The Story Behind the Money

The story behind the money includes the story of your life. It explains what you've been through to get where you are today and why you made certain choices throughout the years.

To tell the story behind the money, it's important to answer questions like the following:

- Why did I choose my career path?
- How did I meet my spouse?
- What did we imagine life would look like for our family?
- What was it like on the day of each child's birth?
- What was the most challenging time in my career?

Answer these questions, and you'll have the story of how you got to where you are today.

Heritage

While the story behind the money relates to your life, heritage is all about your ancestors and your family's origin. It's the story of those who have come before—an understanding of heritage and engaging with past generations. For many people, heritage plays a meaningful role in their self-identity and the overall story of their family.

My grandmother Bridget immigrated from Ireland with only the contents of a wooden suitcase to her name. She braved a rickety boat ride across the ocean, arrived in America at eighteen years old, and created a life from scratch.

When my parents went to Ireland to visit her surviving siblings and their families, they all still talked about Bridget. They walked my parents down the dirt road leading from their family house and said, "This is the point after which we never saw our dear Bridget again."

Even after she had been gone for over fifty-five years, they still called her "dear Bridget." She was thousands of miles away, but she was never forgotten.

My parents told me Bridget's story—about how she met my grandfather on the estate where they were employed. How life was hard but they had my dad and his sister. She lived to be ninety-six years of age. She had several years of knowing my sons, and I told them her story. I have Bridget in me, and now my sons do, too, through her story of an American life.

I take pride in my Irish heritage, but I only developed this pride because those stories of my ancestors were told to me. I also have pride in being a business owner because my dad started his own business. These stories told me my lineage is courageous, triumphant, and does scary things well.

There are families in Texas who are proud of their ranches, which have been passed down through generations and weathered many challenges. When I talk with clients, I solicit these family stories from them because the stories tell me who they are.

When we understand the stories of our families, we can better connect in a meaningful way.

Purpose

The Purpose Pillar includes your family's relationship and connection to your community.

Impact

Intentionality is a powerful component of impact. If I decide not to let the person switch lanes in front of me, I intentionally impact his attitude. On the other hand, if I allow him to switch lanes, I also impact his attitude, but for the better.

The opportunity we have to impact others cannot be understated. So, I challenge you to thoughtfully consider: How do you want to impact the world around you?

"Why is this in a book about wealth?" you might be wondering. I mentioned earlier that you have a powerful moment in time to impact your family, and it starts with you and your *why*. **I believe a positive impact is the most important gift of wealth a human can give to another.** Impact is like dropping a pebble in a pond. You can imagine yourself in the center, dropping the pebble, and in the concentric circles that ripple outward are your family, friends, colleagues, and community. When we impact our thoughts, we impact those around us as well.

To shape your family's impact, involving your children in meaningful charitable projects when they are young and also when they're well into adulthood is so inspiring. I know many families who have supported a particular non-profit for generations because the cause means so much to the members of the family.

Gifting

Time. Talent. Treasure. You may not have time to give from all of those categories, but one may resonate. Serving on nonprofit boards is an excellent way to share leadership skills with community organizations. For some families, gifting to charitable causes is an important component of wealth management. It's a way to build a family's legacy while improving the lives of others.

Gifting does not have to be big and grandiose. Gifting can be in the form of paying for the order of the car behind you in the Starbucks line, anonymously paying for someone's dinner (first responders, perhaps?) in a restaurant, or paying for someone's groceries or heating bill. These are all ways to inspire your kids and grandkids when they are with you to be generous in life.

There are myriad nonprofits, so whatever and however you choose to impact the world around you, the important thing is that it is meaningful to your family to do so.

Have the Right Conversations

Now that I've broken down the Pillars of Wealth, you can use them as a tool to organize your thought processes, get on the same page with your spouse, and figure out how to integrate these crucial aspects into your conversations about wealth with your children.

Your kids need ancestral stories, family traditions, and purpose in the family to connect to the importance of the family inheritance. It can mean more to them than money if you engage them in this way.

The pillars can shape what information you decide to share in your stories and how you choose to deliver it. My parents didn't share stories of their struggles from a "woe is me" mindset. They were joyful and grateful for what they had, but they wanted us to know that life isn't always easy. Sharing their challenges prepared us to face our own.

Don't Let Greed Take a Seat at the Table

Successful families create and sustain family wealth for generations—and it's because they focus on the Pillars of Wealth in some form or fashion. They are governed by purpose, focus on the impact of their wealth, and talk about what's important beyond fiscal wealth.

In other words, they understand and value wealth in all its aspects, and they use it wisely. They think about wealth across generations and are intentional about creating long-lasting inheritances.

You've likely already had a few discussions about inheritance and assets within your family. You've likely witnessed squabbles about it too.

If the only aspect your heirs know about their

> The green-eyed monster of greed rears its ugly head much too often in families. Building strength in family relationships by thinking through the pillars offers a framework for future disagreements about money.

inheritance is the dollar amount or what properties are in the estate, they're likely to be focused only on the fiscal value and nothing else. **By linking estate assets with stories behind wealth and the *why* behind the money, your heirs better understand the importance of shepherding an inheritance.** In fact, they're inspired by it. If you've expressed the *why* behind your assets, heirs can be better stewards of an inheritance because they are connected to it.

Without direction, a family can easily become splintered and directionless. Having money should bring with it peace of mind, but far too often this is not the case simply because the patriarch and matriarch did not spend the time to engage the next generation meaningfully.

Fostering mindfulness, gratitude, and awareness today allows future generations to multiply their inheritance and create their own legacies.

Carrying on the Family Legacy

Heirs should never have anxiety about what to do with an inheritance or how to take care of their parents in the later stage of life. Establishing a plan for success means being clear about the estate, the will, and what provisions are in place for the surviving spouse. Without details, there's simply too much room for confusion.

There's an old saying, "Without a target, you'll miss it every time." Having a plan for the future is better than expecting your heirs to know what to do when they don't even know what to look for.

My parents always had a vision for the future, and they rooted their lives in dreams of a beautiful tomorrow filled with lifting themselves up and out. They dreamed of having many children and making a limitless life possible for us. After we were grown, they admitted the life they had was much richer in experiences than they could have ever imagined.

One of the mottos I heard as they were working long, hard hours was, "Your Mom and I want you to have a better life than we had growing up."

They kept that promise, so much so that their grandchildren also had better lives growing up than my parents. They taught us lessons about the importance of freedom and of always having a dream in focus.

My parents were unified in their Iwhy, and that's how they were able to create a legacy that I continue today through Brennan Wealth Advisors. I am so grateful my dad provided the framework that allows me to guide the wealth aspirations of investors. I have a beautiful life built on top of my parents' strong pillars.

Choose to pass on wealth in all its aspects—your assets, experience, lessons, and purpose—to leave a legacy of your own in the hands of your beloved family.

Actionable Steps

Looking Ahead at Your Financial Future

It's time to develop a future "you" scenario and create a family success plan. We will do that in the next chapter, but as we close this chapter, I have questions for you to ponder:

1. How painful is it to worry about the financial future of your spouse, children, and grandchildren?
2. What would it be like if you didn't worry about them?
3. Would you like a family recipe for success so your kids can avoid some of the hardships you had?
4. What if your spouse knew exactly what to do if you died suddenly?
5. What are you showing your family about financial freedom and independence?
6. Now that you understand each Pillar of Wealth, take a moment to think about your family's definition of wealth. Does it align with your perspective?

Key Concepts

- Wealth is much more than money and physical assets. It's everything you can share with your family, and it can be broken down into four distinct pillars: assets, experience, legacy learning, and purpose. Tying each pillar together at the center lies the heart of your *why*.

- The Assets Pillar includes the physical and financial assets we traditionally think of as inheritances. It also includes intentional values and the power to live life independently, free from debt and financial limitations.

- The Experience Pillar concerns actions and ideas influenced by your *why*. It includes traditions, perspectives, and inspiration you can pass on to heirs.

- The Legacy Pillar involves your family's future and what you'll pass on to the next generation.

- The Purpose Pillar includes your family's relationship and connection to your community. You can build your family's purpose by focusing on the impact you make on others, giving to individuals or institutions, and actions you can take to inspire your community.

- Look for relevant, relatable opportunities to tie your family wealth to each pillar in discussions with your children and spouse. Share stories, create traditions, and lead by example.

- By building a strong understanding of the pillars now, you will increase your family's respect for wealth and can create a meaningful connection to long-lasting inheritances.

3

Plan a Better Life for the Next Generation

Someone is sitting in the shade today because someone planted a tree a long time ago.

—Warren Buffett

Planning a better life for your children and grandchildren isn't about thinking of a day when you won't be around— it's about enjoying the journey as you lay the tracks for an abundant future. That's what the Open Ensō represents, and it's the focus of your next step: preparing the next generation to inherit family wealth.

The motivations underlying your financial goals are what give your assets meaning. Your *why* instills in you a healthy respect for your wealth. You know how hard you worked, and you have a thoughtful plan for the future. But one day in the future when you're gone, hopefully many years from now, will your kids have the same respect?

Leaving inheritances to your children without preparing them properly is like passing them the baton in a footrace when they don't know the direction of the finish line. They might not know the rules of the race, they haven't trained— they may not even know the proper way to receive the baton.

Instead of passing the baton with no training, the most successful families prepare their children by instilling in them a **generational mindset.**

What Is a Generational Mindset?

Guiding children to inherit wealth requires intention as you plan for the future, which is what this chapter is all about. **Intention breeds impact, and impact breeds outcome.**

Your goal now is to instill in your heirs and yourself a long-term vision of wealth centered on values—a generational mindset, as I call it—to guide your family's success.

A generational mindset means thinking about your family's future, both the immediate and far away. It involves asking, "What could our family achieve across generations? What do our heirs need to be equipped to inherit? What do we stand for? What impact could we have on our community or the world? What impact could we have on each other to lead a life of purpose?"

Your family possesses a generational mindset when multiple members are asking these questions and finding the answers together.

As a parent, you've likely asked yourself, "What is my greatest goal for my children?"

Most of us want one thing for our children above all else: for them to have a better life than we've had.

Your wish might be for your kids to have a better childhood than you had or the ability to get a college degree without debt. Perhaps you want them to be happier in their twenties than you were, to have the courage to leave corporate America to establish their own business, or to have fewer adult struggles in life. Most of us share the desire for our children to "have it better," and an important part of your role in that goal is to prepare them to handle wealth.

We want our children to be financially stable, to learn from our lessons, and to benefit when we impart wisdom from our lives. We aim to shape their values, not make their values, and help them grow into the adults they're meant to be. In fact, raising children to be good humans who positively impact humankind could arguably be our best undertaking as parents.

That said, despite a parent's best efforts, many families have one or more adult children who are not on board with shepherding family wealth. Perhaps they aren't trustworthy with money or struggle with personal issues that would make inheriting wealth difficult. Some people need to be protected from themselves, and in these cases, safeguards like establishing trusts to direct assets can be helpful.

Even if you have an adult child who cannot be trusted to manage wealth responsibly, don't let that deter you from involving your grandchildren. Build a connection with them and make them your apprentices. This effort could begin with something as simple as taking them out for ice cream and sharing stories. You have opportunities to pass on wealth in all its aspects, even if it skips a generation.

Create a Multiplier Effect in Your Family

Sharing a generational mindset with your spouse and children is a way for you to create a multiplier effect and achieve much more through your family than any one of you could ever achieve on your own. What does this effect look like in the real world?

In 1962, Sam Walton had a vision to bring prices down for consumers by buying products in bulk. What his business has turned into today—well, that's a great American story. His heirs took up the mantle to work in the family business for generations, and with each generation, they grew his concept to a larger and larger footprint across this nation and the world. According to their corporate website as of August 2022, Walmart employs nearly 1.6 million people in the United States and 2.3 million globally.

Sam Walton was able to instill a generational mindset in his heirs to great effect, resulting in decades of business prosperity and financial security for his family. In my practice, I also hear many stories from clients about a family member who inspired their sound financial habits.

One factor is common in all these stories: the family member who inspired my clients did so by sharing the heart of their *why* and telling stories of how they created wealth by enduring and overcoming hardships. Financial literacy is not only gained through the pragmatic details of investing and saving but also through inspirational storytelling.

Adopting a generational mindset can position your family for long-term happiness and financial success. Keep in mind that the end goal of the generational mindset isn't for everyone to become a millionaire; it's about everyone pursuing the life they want to live and being independently financially resilient.

Your Stories Are Worth Sharing

You might wish that your family had created a multiplier effect for you. The fact is that they did, even if you don't see it. Many incredibly successful entrepreneurs and speakers openly admit to being grateful for a challenging upbringing. Consider these inspirations:

- **Hans Christian Andersen:** The famous writer's story *The Little Match Girl* was inspired by his mother's experience begging in the streets as a young girl.
- **Steve Jobs:** Jobs dropped out of college due to the financial strain on his parents. He was homeless for a while and returned soda bottles for money. Later, he went on to change the consumer-electronics industry as we know it.
- **Andrew Carnegie:** As a child, Carnegie worked in factories and went to sleep at night early to distract himself from his constant hunger. After amassing a fortune in the steel industry, he became one of America's most benevolent philanthropists. He impacted our nation's libraries, education system, and charitable foundations by donating 90 percent of his wealth.
- **J.K. Rowling:** Before her world-famous *Harry Potter* series, Rowling struggled as a single mom on welfare.
- **Madam C.J. Walker:** Walker was the first in her family born free in 1867. She created a line of beauty

products for black women and is recognized as America's first self-made female millionaire.

Hardships create stories worth sharing with the next generation just as often as successes. It's up to you to tell them.

Maybe you look at your young children and think it's too early for them to understand the stories behind your wealth. Or, you might look at your grown children and think it's too late to impact their lives. I'm here to tell you that it's never too early or too late to have these conversations.

Discussions about financial literacy and family wealth are integral, no matter what stage of life your family is in. Raising confident and secure children is not easy, but if left on their own, chances are good that they'll struggle to achieve financial independence. That's why it's so important to take time now to share your stories, values, and lessons.

You will be passing the baton to your children later in life, and your intentional work early on will bring them confidence when they inevitably have big financial decisions to make.

Act with Intention to Make Your Goals a Reality

As with many positive outcomes in life, long-term financial success within a family doesn't happen by accident—it requires us to act. **The role that intention plays in success across generations cannot be overstated.**

To create a family that is financially confident, intentionally passing on skills, values, and a mindset about wealth is where we start. Synchronicity between your family's values and goals is essential for creating a successful generational mindset.

Creating a generational mindset also necessitates a long-term family outlook. The most successful families get results when they create goals backed by the heart of their WHY and followed by actionable intention.

As the leader of Project Family Wealth in your home, helping your children to bridge the gap between their aspirations and financial skills is critical. They need early money habits, an interest in investing, and a foundation in money concepts. You've probably instilled some of these skills naturally with chores, summer jobs, allowances, savings, and money gifted for holidays and birthdays, and they're a great first step.

However, these activities don't translate into financial know-how on their own. Your children should also have their own *why* when setting goals so they have a personal stake in their financial future.

Creating Teachable Opportunities

Build habits with your children when they're young, and those habits will serve them for a lifetime. That's why intentional habit-building is another key component of the Project Family Wealth blueprint.

To demonstrate how to create teachable moments in your household every day, I'd like to share a story from my childhood. When I was growing up, the Sunday newspaper was the only place we had access to stock information. CNBC,

Bloomberg, and Fox Business News did not exist, and there was no ticker tape running at the bottom of the TV screen. Instead of learning about the stock market from the TV or the internet, I learned from my dad.

As the firstborn in my family, I was inseparable from my dad. We did everything together: mowed the lawn, cleaned the car, painted the house, and even reviewed stock updates. On Sunday mornings, when he read the financial section of the newspaper, I looked at it with him.

At eleven years old, I didn't understand that stock was equity in a company. It was too big of a concept, so my dad had me find companies that I knew, like Coca-Cola®, McDonald's®, Mobil™ (where he worked at the time), and Mattel®.

Each Sunday, we hunted for those companies in the paper, wrote down their share prices, and pretended that I bought the stocks. The next Sunday, we looked at those same stocks again. If the stock price of Mattel was up, we celebrated because he explained how I made money. If Mattel was down, he told me how we could buy more shares because they went on sale.

This tradition was how my dad brought the concept of markets and investing to my understanding. Now, we weren't *actually* buying the shares, but it was an incredibly valuable mentoring activity. Our Sunday stock game created the foundation for my lifelong journey of good financial habits. My dad didn't just give me financial knowledge but a sense of confidence and a grounded perspective. I've never worried about volatility because if the market went up or down, I knew what to do in both situations.

This perspective served as a powerful early lesson for me. I'll forever remember the time spent with my dad and will hold cherished memories of our Sunday stock games in my heart and mind. His teaching will always impact my life because he gave me a mindset that has created decades of prosperity for my family and me. When my sons were old enough, this, too, became a game we played. Today as teenagers, they track the stocks they own in a stock app on their phones, and we talk about events that potentially impact those companies.

Similarly, you can have a significant impact on your children's and grandchildren's financial habits and perspectives. It's never too late or too early to educate and prepare those who will carry on your legacy. My dad taught me about stocks when I was young and let that knowledge grow with me, but even if your kids are older, you can still find ways to connect with them and teach your grandkids.

No matter how old your children are, it's important that you start having these conversations. However, before you wheel a whiteboard into the living room, remember that the most effective teaching opportunities are relatable. There's no need for a lecture: your teaching can consist of simple and memorable lessons.

How to *Not* Lose Your Kids' Attention

Most parents don't set out to raise entitled children, but somehow it happens. What's the first step to avoid this outcome?

Remember that we, as parents, are the source of our kids' solid foundation, and it starts with us teaching personal responsibility. The real challenge is conveying these vital lessons in a way that won't lull your kids to sleep.

Perhaps you're ready to impart some knowledge, but you're not sure how to create relatable financial lessons. To give you some ideas, here are a few examples to consider.

To get our kids thinking about the future, my husband and I decided to take the game approach because most kids can relate to playing games. **Having fun—with money lessons thrown in—is more effective than a serious sit-down.** Moreover, this approach can teach kids about the real world because, in most games, like Monopoly®, the goal is to be the accumulator.

If you need some convincing that the "fun approach" works, think back to high school: what are the experiences you remember? How many fun activities, like football games, dances, or classes with your favorite teacher, stand out in your memories?

You can probably recall more of the fun, relatable activities than the serious, academic ones. **The goal of teaching kids is to capture the engaging nature of games while sharing real, valuable knowledge.**

Your kids don't need to be ready to ace a pop quiz on technical financial terms. Instead, aim for them to learn and build on the fundamentals. It only took a few weeks of looking at the stock pages with my dad for me to run out early each Sunday morning to grab the financial section. It's all about getting the young people in your life excited about being lifetime accumulators of wealth.

Actionable Step: The Family Activity Board

A brilliant idea for teaching the value of money came from a pair of my clients who wanted to spur their children to be proactive when helping around the house. The couple created a Family Activity Board, or as they called it, the FAB.

Every week, they pinned numerous pieces of paper to the FAB, each with a task and how much completing that task would be worth. Their activity board included tasks like the following:

- Unload the dishwasher ($5)
- Rake and bag leaves ($10)
- Take the dog for a walk ($5)
- Prepare the table for game night ($5)
- Dust and vacuum the house ($15)

Brilliant, right? The FAB proved to be such a teachable exercise that pretty soon, all three children were asking, "What else can we do?"

The best part of replicating this activity with your children or grandchildren is that you can make it your own by customizing the tasks and payments to fit the needs of your family.

As your children grow, you can introduce age-appropriate activities to teach them new skills. By the time they become teenagers, they'll likely be ready for more responsibility. Establishing a bank account and having a debit card teaches important lessons on money management. Taking your kids inside the bank to set up the account is the beginning of their journey, and you get the chance to demonstrate how they should interact with bank personnel. Adding the bank's app to their phone and yours (so you can monitor how they spend money) helps them understand that they can't buy things they can't afford.

When my sons went to college, the next step was to get them a credit card with a low maximum credit limit. From there, we taught them the importance of a FICO® score. Now, we treat our FICO scores like a game: we sit down, check our credit card apps, and see who has the best score.

By making a competition out of credit scores, my husband and I reinforce the importance of maintaining good credit habits. More importantly, we can do this without falling into parental nagging that risks sparking our children's annoyance—or worse, their indifference.

Tailor Lessons to Fit Your Child's Life Stage

As you guide your family in adopting a generational mindset, it's important to adapt your approach so it's age-appropriate. **During each decade of our children's lives, there's something new to learn about wealth.** As their parent and mentor, your objective is to lead by example at every stage. But it's challenging for us to understand what they need to know and when they need to know it.

To bring things into perspective, I've created a Life Stage Blueprint™ that highlights the most important financial lessons at each stage for you to share with your heirs.

Age Ten to Twenty

- Stage 1: Excitement about investing
    - At this life stage, your kids don't need to learn financial terminology and jargon, like earnings per share. What's most important is getting them excited about being lifetime accumulators of wealth.
    - For now, simply becoming interested in investing will put them on the right track.
    - This decade is when they should learn to manage a savings account, checking account, and investment account. They should also learn how to earn money by having a job.

Age Twenty to Thirty

- Stage 2: Learning financial independence and developing smart money habits
  - ○ Between the ages of twenty and thirty, your children learn how to be on their own financially. They're developing good money habits, setting short-term goals and achieving them, paying off credit cards monthly, and keeping a good credit rating.
  - ○ These are the years that provide—and require—the biggest financial lessons. Managing oneself financially is the key to living an independent life free of financial worry.
  - ○ A big lesson to be learned as investors during this time is this: the way we win the money game is by concentrating on the concept of time *in* the market, not tim*ing* the market. At this stage, many people chase being rich instead of developing grounded practices that create long-term results. They get caught up trying to time the market—whiplash selling and buying—and let smart investing practices fall by the wayside.

Age Thirty to Forty

- Stage 3: Serious goal-setting and financial planning.
  - ○ Between thirty and forty is when serious goal-setting starts. This is when parents can encourage financial planning by sharing with their children what they did in their thirties and forties—for example, how difficult it was

to budget for diapers *and* invest in a 401(k), but why it was worth it.

o Building equity and ownership by investing in the future is a key lesson in this stage. Putting a 20 percent down payment when buying their first house, investing the maximum in their 401(k) plan, and driving their automobiles long after the car payment is complete are all smart moves.

Age Forty to Fifty

- Stage 4: Preparation for the long-term future.
    - o At forty to fifty, preparation for retirement and protecting family wealth is the most important goal. There is no longer time to put off investing and preparing for retirement—it's already knocking on the door.
    - o At this stage, your adult children are fully financially independent, but the lessons they've learned have built the foundation they have now.
    - o Adding insurance to protect financial goals yet to be achieved, visiting with a financial advisor to create a financial plan, and putting in order estate documents like a will and directives are all part of this stage.
    - o This is also a time in their life when they may have questions about your financial preparedness. Share with them the planning you have done to live your best retirement years free from worry.

Your children are unique individuals, and the life stages are not always as clear-cut as they are laid out above. **One fact is certain: good habits start early.**

You might find that your child is ready to tackle financial subjects in their late teens, that most people encounter in their early twenties. However, by generally following the Life Stage Blueprint and using it to guide your conversations, you can ensure that you're teaching your children good money habits throughout their lives.

Create a Family Motto

A motto is a phrase that you frequently use because it encapsulates your beliefs and values. Chances are you have a motto or two already—something like, "I can do hard things," or, "If you fall down, dust yourself off and get right back up." Or, as we say in Texas, "If you fall off, get right back in the saddle."

In addition to creating age-appropriate teachable moments with your family, you can instill a generational mindset by defining and sharing your personal mottos. Better yet, have your kids get involved and create a family motto together.

When our kids were young, my husband and I would tell our sons before they left the house, "You're the only you God made, so take good care of yourself." Even after their teenage years end and many times hearing, "I know, Mom, I know," we still tell them this.

Later, we wanted them to be prepared for emergencies when they had their own money to manage. We taught them the motto, "Always be prepared." We didn't want them to tune us out if we directly told them that they needed to have money in the bank for emergencies. Emergencies don't ring true for kids.

Remember, for financial lessons to stick and amplify over time, they have to be relatable. **Whether you're defining a motto or creating a teachable activity, phrasing the core idea in a way that is understandable for your child is best.**

If you're teaching your children to "expect the unexpected," find kid-level emergencies that they can prepare for and understand, like making them responsible for maintaining their game console or their pet goldfish. If their game controller breaks or the goldfish dies, it's important that they are the ones to replace it. My husband and I found that when our sons knew they would have to pay for certain things, they took better care of those items.

When one of your children does well in money management and caring for their possessions, celebrate. As their parent, your praise goes the furthest in cementing good habits.

Learning to be responsible with money early is a crucial step toward financial resilience in adulthood. When your kids and grandkids get older and have their own pets, they'll have to be prepared for unexpected visits to the veterinarian. When they have their own car, they'll have to be prepared to buy tires. When they have their own house, they'll have to be able to pay for new floors if the water heater breaks.

The experience of having saved for small emergencies in your child's youth gives them the know-how to confidently and independently tackle their adult-scale financial emergencies.

Successful Families Share Mottos

Have you ever wondered how some families seem to move in unison? It's as if they are all singing from the same sheet of music—they're able to work together to reach their goals.

I've had the opportunity to serve client families of all kinds in my career. This exposure has afforded me the ability to study successful and not-so-successful family practices, one of which is that successful families tend to share mottos. Not only do they agree on which mottos to repeat, but they also use their shared mottos to guide their decisions.

There's no better example of family mottos in action than family ranches. In Texas, we have many family ranches and farms that have been running for generations. At the core of the success of these legacy ranches is one thing: a united family mindset. These families have common values passed on through a motto that everyone knows. A motto I am accustomed to hearing is, "My grandfather's father, my grandfather, and father are all buried here. I will be, too."

People who value this motto honor the generations past. They come together with their family members around a common goal—to preserve the family's land and business—and each individual contributes. The family unit is a unified business, which is why the successful ranchers and farmers don't have to sell parcels of their land generation after generation to stay afloat.

You already know that one of my family's mottos is "Expect the unexpected." That motto has manifested in our kids' preparedness and confidence as they entered adulthood. What family mottos do you have?

If you're struggling to identify your family motto, ask your kids what common lessons or phrases you've told them throughout their lives. You might have already created a motto without even realizing it.

When thinking about your motto, does it line up with the *why* that you identified in Chapter One? If not, creating a motto that does is a good place to start.

Storytelling Is at the Heart of the Generational Mindset

Equally important to *what* you say about wealth and *when* you say it is *how* you say it. Mottos can only convey so much—sometimes you need a longer format. To this end, you'll find that storytelling is one of your most valuable tools when it comes to communicating lessons and instilling a generational mindset in your children.

Consider the following scenario: you're a prolific accumulator. You go to work, take home your paycheck, and invest and save your money as you move toward achieving your goals. You don't talk to your family about your 401(k), how much life insurance you have, or why you chose to start a business. You don't explain why you live where you live, why you chose a certain financial advisor, or how your spouse will be financially able to live when you are gone. You internalize the reasoning and research behind the big decisions that affect your entire family.

Even though they've witnessed the outcome of your decisions, your family members are not truly learning lessons if you leave out the *why* behind your decisions. For your spouse and kids to understand the decisions you make and not worry whether you're prepared for the future, it's important that you articulate how you're accumulating wealth and what you're doing with it.

In fact, not sharing the reasoning behind financial decisions is the biggest mistake I see in families. When only one person holds all the financial knowledge, it's a big risk for the other members of the family. My firm often receives calls from clients asking if we know the password to a home computer, whether their father had a life insurance policy, where monthly income will come from, or who the beneficiaries are on investments.

Having seen the stress and confusion this causes in families, I encourage you to tell the whole story behind your choices. By explaining your thought process, your loved ones can understand your financial journey from start to finish. They'll know what to do in case the worst happens unexpectedly, and you're no longer around to provide answers.

Telling the stories behind your life decisions can be a powerful experience—both for sharing your knowledge and for bringing your family closer together. Your thirties, when you had two kids, shared one car and could afford to vacation every other year, might just be life to you, but to your children, it's an invaluable learning opportunity.

While you pass on wisdom, keep in mind that you're not copying and pasting your money principles; you're helping your children develop their own. As times and markets have changed within your lifetime, you've likely had to shift your money principles from those of your parents, and your children will do the same. Your responsibility is to set your children up to face these shifts confidently and successfully.

Your life experiences reveal the core of who you are, your mindset, values, and goals. If given the chance, those life experiences can become a legacy through your children.

Intentionally Shape Your Family's Future

Wealth is more than money, and it's worth imparting it in all its aspects.

At some point, all children reflect on their upbringing and want more. This desire is partly human, partly our society, and partly our parents. As parents, we all hope to create a good life for our children and inspire them to go beyond and above our expectations. But it's easy to be swept up in the pursuit of wealth, to be consumed by "keeping up with the Joneses" and put it above what's most important: our values and morals.

We are responsible for helping our children shape their own *why* by intentionally guiding our family's attitude toward money. Our sole purpose isn't to be rich. If it happens, terrific, but it's not where our values come to life.

As you work to impart a generational mindset to your family, I encourage you to imagine the future. What milestones do you want your family to hit in the next ten, twenty, and thirty years?

Now, ask yourself what has to happen for you to be happy with what your family achieved together. It's time to figure out how to implement a generational mindset that will support your family. What do you want your multiplying effect to be? How will you create a lasting impact that will give your family the knowledge and freedom to create beautiful and fulfilling lives?

All it takes is commitment, intentionality, and clarity about your financial values.

As the financial head of your family, your role is to inspire a lifetime of responsible wealth pursuits in your family and the following generations.

Be intentional about your family's values and long-term goals. Choose a motto (or several) that captures those principles and create teachable moments for your children. When you bring it all together and get your family moving in the same direction, you'll know you're living with a generational mindset.

Actionable Steps

To help you define your family's mottos, start by answering the following questions.

What beliefs and values are important to you as a family?

_____

_____

_____

_____

What phrases or lessons have you repeated to your children over the years?

_____

_____

_____

_____

Are there any "words to live by" that your parents shared with you that you still follow today?

_____

_____

_____

_____

Imagine your family in five years. What impact would you like to have made during this time?

_____

_____

_____

_____

Key Concepts

- Leaving your children an inheritance that they will manage wisely and amplify, not squander, is like passing them a baton in a relay race—it requires planning, training, and intentional habit-building to be successful. If you don't prepare them, who will? Adult children want to carry out their parents' intentions. Give them that opportunity.

- To prepare your children to manage the family wealth, instill in them a generational mindset. By living with a generational mindset, your family has the opportunity to achieve much more across generations than any one person might do on their own. Consider how founder Sam Walton and his heirs grew Walmart into the international juggernaut it is today.

- To create financial confidence within your family, it's important to be intentional. Set goals that align with your *why*, share these with family members, and act to bring them to fruition.

- Create teachable opportunities to develop good financial habits in your children. The most effective lessons are fun and relatable—try making age-appropriate games out of simple financial concepts.

- To guide your children toward responsible financial values, adopt a family motto (or several) that encapsulates your beliefs.

- Don't underestimate the power of storytelling as a vehicle to share knowledge and values with your family. You'll teach your children important lessons, and it can bring you closer together as a family.

4

What Your Family Thinks about Wealth

There is an old-fashioned word for the body of skills that emotional intelligence represents: character.

—Daniel Goleman

"Tone at the top," which refers to an organization's values as they're set from the leadership down, is important in any organization. It educates the culture and ultimately impacts the outcome produced by its members. Family is no different.

By defining the *why* behind your financial goals, you have begun the process of shaping family culture. Now, you're ready for the next step in Project Family Wealth: getting buy-in from your family.

There are two parts to this process: communication and education. Communicating your *why* to your family tells them the direction, and education tells them how. If you tell your adult children, "Take care of Mom when I'm gone," without educating them on how, your plans may fall through.

Consider the myriad questions they could have. Where does the monthly income come from? Where are your investments and life insurance? Who is your financial advisor? Where do you bank? What is the password to your computer and online banking apps? Where are your latest estate documents?

Your heirs don't know what they don't know. Preparing them for you to pass the baton successfully is job number one.

That's why it's so important to communicate views on wealth early on in your children's lives. When you support your decision-making with *why* and *how*, your vision can inspire your entire family. That's what this chapter is about— the heart of your *why* inspiring their hearts.

How Your Spouse Thinks About Money

Teamwork is an ideal first step in creating a framework for good family conversations. Getting you and your spouse on the same page about family wealth is key.

An important factor contributing to the success of Project Family Wealth is bringing your spouse's perspective into the picture.

Typically there is one spouse most interested in money who directs financial decisions, and one spouse not so interested. A good approach to begin your discussion with your spouse is with the *why* of your goal setting. Forget the finances of it all. Get to the heart of it. Why do you want her involved? To make sure she's okay if something happens to you? To be an example for your two daughters? So you can dream together about the future? So she won't worry about the future?

Whatever your reasons, it's essential that you both understand and respect each other's viewpoint. Why has she not been involved in planning for the future? Could it be that she thinks she doesn't possess the right financial skills? Maybe your financial advisor doesn't address her when she goes to meetings with you. Does she believe you should make the decisions since you are the primary income earner? Tone at the top starts with both spouses leading Project Family Wealth.

It's also necessary for your children to see you working together. If your children see that your spouse is on board, they'll be more likely to be on board, too. If you're not aligned, this could become the reason you don't get family buy-in.

Having both parents present a unified front is yet another secret of successful families. Families that create long-lasting inheritances have children who grow up to be self-sufficient, financially independent individuals. It all starts with both spouses being on the same page about money, values, and long-term goals.

Complementary Viewpoints: Financial IQ and Financial EQ

To get on the same page, it helps to understand how your viewpoints differ. How might your spouse think about money differently than you?

When it comes to perspectives on finance, there are usually two primary viewpoints: Financial Intelligence Quotient™ (IQ) and Financial Emotional Quotient™ (EQ). Although these aren't necessarily gendered traits, based on my years of experience as a financial advisor, I've seen that the patriarch of the family tends to operate from Financial IQ, and the matriarch tends to operate from Financial EQ. These are unique and necessary perspectives that, when combined, present a unified force to lead the family.

Financial IQ is a performance-based perspective concerned with the *how* of wealth. Patriarchs of the family typically want to know facts and tactics: how much money they need in retirement, how long investments will take to grow, what investing will cost, and the performance track record of recommended investments.

Financial EQ is a results-based perspective or the *why* behind financial goals. It is the awareness of the motivations behind the use of money and the achievement of a goal. The matriarch usually wants to know, "What will this money help us do?"

She's most interested in the personal impact of financial decisions. For example, an investment might pay for the grandchildren's college education so they graduate without student loans; a retirement plan may offer lifetime income to prevent running out of money; or a charitable trust may allow philanthropic contributions to improve the community.

These two perspectives, Financial IQ and EQ, are the patriarch and matriarch's superhero strengths. When they come together, this balanced outlook is the key to family financial resilience. The viewpoints are not competing or overpowering each other but collaborating to create a grounded financial outlook. **When Financial IQ and EQ come together, this relationship expands the family's**

perspective on money and communicates its impact and importance. This is the powerful heart of the *why* that inspires the entire family. This is leadership.

Once these are balanced and you and your spouse have a strong financial foundation to operate from, you can engage your children in the conversation.

Embrace Each Family Member's Perspective

Connecting is about understanding skill sets, personalities, and desires. The next step to sharing your *why* is understanding how everyone is wired so that you can connect with family members in a meaningful way.

Respecting and embracing different personalities and perspectives, which create a rich family culture, helps everyone feel like part of the process. Furthermore, when you understand what others are thinking, you can address the worries that each individual may have about money.

Without this essential step, a husband might not realize that his wife is worried about how to make specific decisions about the future when he is gone. Parents might not recognize that their children worry about providing long-term care if it's necessary. Adult children may not know that their parents are concerned if enough money has been set aside for the grandchildren's college education. Everyone worries about money. Everyone. The key is to talk about it. Get it out in the open.

Only by hearing these worries can you address them in your financial planning. Getting concerns into the open prevents them from snowballing into larger issues in the future, and it also allows for each family member to be heard.

The most reliable way to free yourself and your family from the burden of worry is by having a financial plan. The root of most worry is that major issues are unattended to, avoided, and not discussed.

Certainly, it's easier to avoid uncomfortable topics with family, but that avoidance can complicate the legacy we hope to leave and may even jeopardize family relationships. If we picture the heart of your *why* as the engine, the "tough stuff" is the chassis. Unless the chassis is stable, we won't be able to move forward and reach our destination. In other words, we must address the tough stuff to give our family stability.

Uncover Your Family's Worries

Every family has their set of topics they don't want to talk about. Patriarchs of the family worry about what will happen to their spouse when it comes time for them to step into the role of financial decision-maker. Women worry about handling money when their husband passes. Adult children worry about overstepping boundaries when they ask about the plans for the future. If these worries don't get discussed, no one is empowered to take control of their future.

Many families share the same concerns about money:

- Will my spouse know what to do financially when I am gone?
- Who can my spouse trust to assist in making financial decisions?
- Will my adult children be able to manage an inheritance?
- Are my parents financially prepared for a long retirement?
- Who in our family will make financial decisions for Mom and Dad when they cannot?
- Who will be the executor to direct estate assets?

- How will we pay health costs?
- How will special assets (cars, land, houses, art, jewelry, and furniture) be directed to inheritors?

After everyone gets their worries out in the open, you can decide how to address them and move forward.

Actionable Step: Personality Assessments

Many successful family meetings begin with a team-building activity. If you have not yet given your family the opportunity to participate in a personality assessment, this is a great way to lead a family discussion. Online personality tests like the Kolbe A™ Index, StrengthsFinder®, and DiSC® Assessment are quick and easy. These assessments facilitate your conversations by giving insight into individual differences and strengths. Most importantly, it will become apparent how meaningful each member's contribution to Project Family Wealth can be. Knowing each other in this way will help your family operate well, understand preferences, and honor learning styles.

Knowing yourself is valuable, but the real value is in reading everyone else's results and getting an inside look at the motivations behind their thoughts and reactions. The goal is to understand and love every member of your family for their unique personalities and create a cohesive, unified plan for Project Family Wealth.

Be Aware of What You're Teaching Your Children

Something else to keep in mind when passing on a generational mindset is the importance of perspective. For everything that you have to give (lessons, values, stories, assets, love, and kindness) to be echoed within your family for decades, being intentional with what you're teaching your children is crucial. Your hope is for them to carry that knowledge with them into the next generation.

How are you leading by example, mentoring, and creating strong financial family bonds? Sometimes, it can be as easy as taking your young kids shopping, volunteering together at your favorite charity, or engaging your adult children in a business decision you are making. It's necessary to support these experiences with additional discussions about why we do what we do to prevent possible misunderstandings, as my husband and I learned.

We have always taught our kids that "cash is king" from an early age so that our sons would understand the importance of paying with cash. When we went to the toy store, we would first ask our kids what was on their list so that they developed a sense of prioritization in shopping. Then, we gave our sons a spending limit, usually ten or twenty-five dollars, and let them pick out what they wanted within that budget. At the register, we handed our sons the cash to pay for their toy so that they had the experience of paying. It was also important for them to interact with the cashier on their own.

Simple acts like this—saying hello to the cashier, handing them the cash, getting change back, taking the receipt, and saying thank you and goodbye—all had a powerful impact early on in building their confidence and knowledge.

We made it a point to give our kids a budget because many parents tell their kids that they can get just one toy—maybe two if they're really good. The problem with this is that when a kid has no understanding of prices and they see aisle after aisle of toys, they don't understand why they're limited.

We wanted our sons to understand that money isn't an unlimited resource because it sets up an unrealistic relationship between money and the value of purchased items. Our toy store ritual was our way of teaching our sons that being responsible with money means buying things in moderation.

I thought that this lesson was enough, but I wasn't aware of just how closely my sons watched our relationship with money. A trip to the grocery store with my son Cameron made me realize that I needed to adapt my teaching methods.

Cameron was eight years old, and at this point, his knowledge of money was mostly shaped by the toy store. At the toy store, my husband and I had emphasized the importance of moderation, but when we shopped for groceries, what did he watch us do?

I didn't just buy one thing, but a lot of things—I filled up the grocery cart. From his eight-year-old height, he was at eye level with every item that I picked up, and I can't imagine how full that cart must have looked to him.

In my mind, I had compartmentalized necessities from wants, but I hadn't explained that hierarchy of needs to Cameron yet. As I shopped, he probably thought, *Why can't I do this at the toy store? She's filling the cart with bread, vegetables, and fruit, so why can't I fill my cart with Legos®, action figures, and video games?*

On top of that, he had only ever paid for his toys with dollar bills, so when he saw me pull out a debit card at the register, he must have thought it was magic.

After we loaded the groceries in the car and were driving home, Cameron asked, "Mom, where do you get that red card?"

"What red card?"

"The red card you put in the machine at the grocery store. You didn't pay cash."

"Well, I did pay cash. That was my debit card."

"Can I get one, too?" he asked. "That way, I'll be able to buy as much of anything that I want."

At that moment, I realized my mistake: I had only been teaching the Financial IQ of how we paid and not including the Financial EQ, which explains why we spend money the way we do. There was a huge gap in his knowledge of money that I didn't even realize was affecting his understanding.

Cameron didn't yet understand the EQ of money management, but he understood the IQ. He understood the concept of cash, but because I didn't explain that the same concept carried through to my debit card, which he saw me use at the grocery store and restaurants, he thought it was magic.

After this, my husband and I explained that the reason we couldn't load up a cart with toys and games and other fun things was that we had to prioritize our needs first, like getting gas for the car and putting food on the table. I passed on the stories that my parents had given me about money management. When they were first married, they had a physical way of inventorying their money. After each paycheck came in, they would divide that money into separate envelopes labeled rent, food, gas, and fun. This was their budgeting system. And it worked. Even though, at that point I was too young to watch and understand, they made a point of telling me that story often later in life.

Consider the story about my son and the debit card, and think about what lessons you have to share with your kids. What can you teach them?

No matter how old your children are, there are appropriate lessons that can further their financial education.

If you can't think of any stories, don't worry. There's no need to pressure yourself to have personal examples because finding a way to communicate that knowledge is enough. If you don't have your own story for every lesson, borrowing other people's stories or examples can work just as well.

Parenting Never Ends

Contemplating lessons to share with your children, whether young or grown, brings to light a reality we all live with: parenting never ends. It's a beautiful lifelong gift parents have of giving all we have in the way of lessons, values, family stories, assets, and traditions.

It doesn't stop when your kids turn eighteen, go to college, and move out. There are always opportunities to teach financial stewardship.

Your kids might not ask for direction and leadership, but they will look to you for guidance their entire lifetime.

When I opened up my first office, I channeled my dad as much as possible and thought about what I had watched him do when he opened up his very first office. I was just sixteen years old, but I still remembered the wisdom I gained by observing him. I didn't realize at the time how brave he was to leave corporate America to start his own business with four children under the age of sixteen. Looking back, I am inspired by what courage it took.

It's also important to share stories of a major challenge or even a mistake you experienced in life when it is appropriate for your child to understand. It's natural for parents to want to hide setbacks from their kids, but they miss out on valuable teaching opportunities by doing so. I like to call these discussions "I remember when" stories:

> *I remember when I got my first driving ticket. I remember when my first job didn't pay well. I remember when I didn't know if my business would survive COVID shutdowns. I remember when I didn't know which career major to study in college and how scary adult life seemed.*

Sharing your stories will help them when they experience their own setbacks.

Remember, you are a rockstar in your children's eyes, and letting them in on some of your life's challenges can be extremely rewarding for both of you. These teachable moments are priceless in creating deeper family relationships. There is value in life lessons—more value than you can buy from a university class because you've lived the lesson.

By sharing your firsthand knowledge, your children will have an example of how to handle problems. Moreover, they'll begin the very important life habit of turning their mistakes into learning.

The most meaningful lessons in life you likely learned from experience or from your parents. Rather than let your kids start from scratch, use this moment in time to pass on what you know. You can accelerate their natural intake of this knowledge and give them a trusted person (you) to come to when life is challenging.

Beyond saving them from painful missteps, your kids will also cherish these discussions because they'll see that you trusted them with personal information. In turn, they'll know that they can share with you, too.

When we become parents, we often rush to squeeze in as many lessons as possible, which can create a one-sided conversation. Instead, it's worth making space to hear from our kids.

Listening is just as important as telling. Be interestED instead of interestING when spending time with your family.

Teach Real-World Money Lessons

You know your kids better than anyone else, so you know when your kids are going to be ready to understand certain financial lessons. Some kids are interested in personal finance when they're in high school, but some aren't interested until after they graduate college.

No matter your children's age, what's most important is that you've built trust with them and shared your experiences along the way so that they can rely on that knowledge. When they're ready to hear it, let them in on your thought process. Explain why you're refinancing the house or why you made certain decisions in your will. When it comes to money, the more transparency, the better.

If your children are still young, consider setting up debit and savings accounts for them. Then, pass the reins to them when they're ready. If you do online banking, have their account in your lineup so that you can advise about their spending habits.

Once they understand good spending and saving practices, set up an investment account and get them engaged. Take them out for milkshakes and go over some of the stocks that they own. The goal is to chart a course for a good financial future while also giving them the freedom to learn through experience.

Investment accounts are important for kids to experience early on. The average age for when people begin to invest varies, but most Americans don't invest until entering their thirties. If only they had parents who introduced them to investing early on, they would be able to understand that it's time IN the market that matters most, not TIMING the market.

The Rule of 72

The Rule of 72 is a tool that tells us how quickly we can double our money based on how much we expect to earn from the savings or investing account. You divide seventy-two by the expected return rate to calculate how many years it will take your money to double.[3]

If you put your money in the bank and—fingers crossed—expect a 2 percent return, it would take thirty-six years for your money to double because seventy-two divided by two is thirty-six.

$$72 \div 2 = 36$$

---

[3] The Rule of 72 demonstrates a mathematical principle. It does not illustrate any investment products and does not show past or future performance of any specific investment.

Instead, if you decided to put your money into a bond that earns 6 percent, the Rule of 72 tells us that it will take twelve years to double your money in that bond.

$$72 \div 6 = 12$$

If your investment timeline is longer, meaning you can take more risk, you could invest in stocks that historically have earned 10 percent, which means it would take just over seven years to double your money.

Rule of 72

72	72	72
÷ 2	÷ 6	÷10
36	12	7.2

When investors start to think about time in the market, the Rule of 72 demonstrates why the length of time is the main factor. If you decide that you're going to retire in twelve years, wouldn't you like to give your money the opportunity to double twice instead of once?

The Rule of 72 drives home the point to select the most appropriate investment for your time horizon. Obviously, it's no guarantee that investors will earn a steady return since markets change from moment to moment. It's a simple calculation to assist in decision-making. This is why, in our thirties, forties, and fifties, we should consider investing in our 401(k) and in stocks to give our money more time in the market and an opportunity to double quicker.

Most people who aren't aware of the importance of time in the market realize their mistakes in their fifties, worry about their retirement, and invest fearfully. They try to time the market by selling when it's low and buying when it's high, which is the opposite of what they should be doing. No one has ever perfected the ability to time the market, and if there were such a person, we'd all be lining up to talk with her or him.

Teach the importance of time in the market to your children to allow them to get ahead in life instead of them learning it on their own too late.

When your child is an adult and on their own, it will be easier for them to navigate significant investments for the future and make big purchases like homes and cars. They'll also understand the importance of having a good credit score, which is essential for preferred interest rates when borrowing and even getting a job in certain industries like financial services, the military, accounting, law enforcement, and mortgage loan originators.

Their credit score, investments, and spending habits will be important for the rest of their lives, so it's never too early to get a head start. These habits are like riding a bike: once they know how to use them, they'll never forget.

Success Depends on Balance

Figuring out the right, balanced approach between your Financial IQ and Financial EQ is the key to establishing a generational mindset in your family. Too much of either perspective stalls the process, but the right balance is akin to a family superpower. It's what separates families with long-lasting legacies from families whose financial wealth dissipates in a generation or two.

To secure your place in the first category, it's important to find a balance between you and your spouse and a balance within yourself. Aim to understand both the Financial IQ—the how—of your personal approach to money and the EQ—the why. You've already begun this journey by exploring the *why* behind your financial goals; now it's time to break down your relationship with money further. Are your Financial IQ and EQ balanced?

When I meet with spouses, I always suggest a balance so that each spouse has a stake in the financial decisions that reflect them. If the financial goals of a family or couple reflect only one person's objectives, wants, and desires, it becomes very hard to get the family's support. Instead, when goals reflect both spouses, this cohesive approach makes achieving the goals so much easier.

When you create a grounded perspective as an individual and a family, both Financial IQ and Financial EQ balance each other out. You're smart with your money, but you also know how to enjoy life and invest in your family. The right balance strengthens the foundation for the next step in Project Family Wealth: the four pillars of family legacy that you will build.

Key Concepts

- You have a powerful moment in time to communicate your views on wealth with your family.

- There are two predominant ways people tend to think about money: the Financial IQ (the *how* behind the money) and the Financial EQ (the *why* behind the money).

- It's important to understand whether your spouse is stronger in Financial IQ or EQ. Respect and value their way of thinking because you both bring a critical component to the table for long-term financial success.

- Use personality tests, like the Kolbe A Index, to better understand your family members and to start productive conversations.

- Be aware of what you're teaching your children, both intentionally and unintentionally. Your children are always watching and learning from your examples.

- Share stories of your successes *and* mistakes with your family. Letting your children learn from your mistakes helps them enter adult life prepared for financial success. Ideally, they can avoid some of the hardships and struggles you've experienced by heeding your advice.

- Listening is just as important as telling. Be interested instead of interesting.

- Use real-world activities and responsibilities, like a savings account, to teach your children about money.

- Your family's generational success depends on balancing Financial IQ and Financial EQ. Recognize and value what you and your spouse each bring to the table and strive for a happy medium between prudent spending and enjoying life. Define your vision for your family's future and then find a way to fund it.

5

It Takes a Team

*Give people enough guidance to make the decisions
you want them to make. Don't tell them what to do,
but encourage them to do what is best.*

—Jimmy Johnson, Dallas Cowboys Head Coach

Now that you've taken some time to define the *why* behind your financial goals, understand your family's perspectives on money, and consider your wealth in all its aspects, it's time to put it together.

How do you and your loved ones work as a team to create long-lasting inheritances that turn family wealth into *generational* family wealth?

The answer is by playing to your family members' strengths. To illustrate what I mean, picture yourself attending a football game. All around you, people look thrilled to be at the stadium on a beautiful day. Cheerleaders flip on the sidelines, and you hear the band playing just loudly enough to be heard over the roar of the crowd.

It's time for the game to begin. The announcer calls out your team's name, and you watch for the players to run onto the field—but wait, something isn't right.

Only the quarterback runs out of the tunnel and onto the field. There's no way the quarterback can play the whole game by himself (despite what some of them might think). The game can only be won when there's a team effort. As it turns out, generational wealth is the same.

Each person in your family plays a necessary role in the family's wealth aspirations, and every role is valuable. To succeed at creating generational wealth, it's important to apply everybody's strengths and put each person in the role best suited for them.

Imagine now that the rest of the football team runs onto the field and takes their places, but their roles are scrambled. The star quarterback has swapped places with the kicker, and the linemen are now wide receivers. Even if the whole team is on the field, they would still lose the game because each player's skills aren't properly utilized.

Each player on a football team earned their position because of their unique strengths and talents. The quarterback knows how to execute plays, the kicker repeatedly makes field goals, and so on. If the coach doesn't inspire and use each player's unique strengths, the team loses.

When creating a financial plan for the future, putting the right people in the right roles is crucial to bringing out your family's full potential and setting the stage for generational wealth.

No one can create an indelible family legacy—or win a football game—all on their own.

Building on the Generations

Before we explore the various roles involved in managing family wealth—and which role suits each of your family members—it can be helpful to think about the generations that came before. Who set the foundation for the family you have today?

Co-founder of Strategic Coach®, Dan Sullivan, illustrates in his book *Who Not How* how to achieve bigger goals by determining the "Whos" that are necessary for forward progress. I've been a member of Strategic Coach® for years, and this concept is a game-changer in business and family life. Dan urges entrepreneurs to stop asking, "How can I do this?" and instead ask, "Who can do this for me?"

Each of us is an important link in an intergenerational progression of family, and the heart of your *why* has been planted by the generations before you. You are who you are due in part to values, work ethics, stories, assets, traditions, and commitments that were passed on to you, onto which you layered your unique talents and life desires. This is the richness of family.

Your *why* is the culmination of the generations before you. Their stories and decisions have shaped you. That doesn't mean you're a carbon copy of your ancestors, but they're a part of who you are. Your unique talents and life desires are what round out the heart of your *why* and make it your own. Now, it is important for you to ask, "Who in the family can play key roles in Project Family Wealth?"

What was important in the past and what is important to you now shapes what will be important to you in the future. This, in turn, shapes the influence your legacy will have throughout generations.

Your role in this process is to make intentional and meaningful connections between past generations, present generations, and future generations.

You'd be surprised how often finance is tied to stories about family history and tradition. When I meet with clients, only a quarter of the meeting tends to be about finances and money. The rest is about the stories of my client's family: their hopes for their grandkids and children, the hard knocks they've overcome, their decisions to move to another state or change careers, and the impact of it all on their vision for the future. These conversations detail the motivations behind a family's financial goals.

Wealth in all its aspects—not only assets but traditions, perspectives, values, heritage, family stories, purpose, and more—is inextricably linked to long-lasting inheritances. Using the Pillars of Wealth from Chapter Two, you made an inventory of everything you have to pass on to the next generation and organized your gifts into the four areas of wealth.

Now, it's time to consider specific roles within your family to enhance and grow those gifts. I call this step "making important things important."

Once you've done the personality assessments discussed in Chapter Four, the matter of which role suits each family member will become clearer. You may have someone who excels at managing finances, another who loves maintaining traditions and keeping family history, another who wants to expand the family's philanthropic efforts, and another who is skilled at organizing and accountability.

Whether you are a corporate executive, run a family-owned business, operate a family ranch, or desire to manage family money together, the idea is the same. Your role is to connect all of the gifts cascading into the family from previous generations and pass them on to your kids in the best way possible.

> When people can play to their strengths and are in the right role, team synergies happen. When this occurs in a family, it's magic. Successful families understand the importance of everyone pulling in the same direction by using each other's strengths.

Focus on Strengths, Not Weaknesses

When deciding what role each person in your family will play, instead of noting what someone is *not,* focus on their strengths. We all have more strengths than weaknesses, so concentrate on what each person has to offer. Do your family members have specific areas of expertise? Find out everyone's strengths and interests.

If some family members worry they don't have anything to contribute because they're financially inexperienced, remind them that Financial EQ—emotional quotient, or the *why* behind the money—is just as important as Financial IQ—intelligence quotient, or the *what* and *how* behind the money.

For example, someone might not be the person to manage the minute financial details, but they could have a skill set for big-picture thinking, defining philanthropic impact, acting as a family historian, creating meaningful family traditions and gatherings, or ensuring that everyone's motivations align.

The goal of delegating specific roles is to ensure that everyone contributes in the most fulfilling and least stressful way possible.

By understanding everyone's strengths, no one will be forced into a role that's too difficult for them. A football coach would never put a star wide receiver in as a lineman because that's not his strength—maybe he's just not big enough to make the plays happen. He's much more valuable in the right spot where his strengths and abilities lie.

Simply put, your family is a team, and as the coach, your job is to put the right people in the right role.

Name a Single Executor: No More and No Less

Collaboration is key to managing generational wealth, but be aware that some roles need to be taken on by an individual to avoid confusion and conflict.

A football team won't perform well with more than one quarterback on the field calling plays, and it's the same with family wealth. That's why it's important to name only a single executor for your estate.

The executor is the person responsible for carrying out the terms of a will and the wishes of the decedent. They're in charge of resolving any debt the estate may owe, transferring assets to people designated in the will, and fulfilling the last wishes spelled out in the will. Everyone else plays a supporting role.

Think of appointing a single executor as creating a transparent chain of command, one that is discussed premortem with your family. I cannot stress how important this step is in the successful transition of estate assets. Sharing your intentions about the roles each member plays in settling the estate can make the difference between them working cohesively as a team and letting egos and conflict get in the way. Assuming that your adult children will just figure it out together is not a plan, as that rarely goes as expected.

Choosing backup executors is necessary to prepare for all possibilities, but appointing co-executors creates a tug-of-war of responsibilities and decisions that lead to conflict. With co-executors, people step on each other's toes, have unclear responsibilities, and can spend more time arguing than carrying out the directives of the will.

Set your family up for success by choosing a single person as the executor of your will and avoiding unnecessary conflict within your family.

Unfortunately, many people avoid choosing a single executor because deciding who gets the role can be stressful. Parents don't know how to approach this topic with their children, so they avoid the discussion entirely until it's too late.

In an attempt to make everyone equal, some parents name all of their children co-executors because they don't want to hurt feelings or show favoritism. But make no mistake: naming an executor of your will has nothing to do with whom you love or value most. It's about determining who has the capability for the role and who may relieve other siblings who played larger roles earlier, like caring for a sick parent and handling the sale of family real estate.

After all, being named an executor is not a badge of honor; it's a thankless job. It involves mountains of paperwork, time, and difficult decisions. This all becomes more complicated the more people are involved.

Each Role in Family Wealth Has Value

Even without naming co-executors, you can still have an equal division of responsibilities in handling family wealth.

What are these other roles?

Here are some of the more common responsibilities involved in managing an estate, although your family may have more or fewer depending on your unique circumstances:

- Caring for the surviving spouse and organizing healthcare
- Dealing with finances and bills
- Managing property, such as selling the house when it comes time
- Running the family business
- Leading the family's philanthropic efforts
- Planning family get-togethers and ensuring traditions continue

Successful families create a clear division of roles and responsibilities to ensure that every one of these important jobs is handled as efficiently and effectively as possible. A chain of command allows everyone to understand why they were chosen for their role and the duties it entails.

Open dialogue and transparent decision-making around these roles help to avoid hurt feelings. If everyone can understand the *why* behind estate-leadership roles, it creates an immense amount of respect for each role. For example, maybe your son is a doctor, so he's the natural choice to be the power-of-health attorney and deal with any healthcare needs. If your daughter is an accountant, she can handle financial decisions while your son quarterbacks the healthcare responsibility.

When people have clear roles, it prevents them from arguing about who is responsible for what over and over again.

Defined roles also prevent the bystander effect, where no action is taken at all because everyone assumes someone else will step up. In emergency-response training, the best practice is to point at someone specific and instruct them to call 911; otherwise, everyone hesitates to take action, and the call is delayed, costing precious time. By determining roles in your family early on, your planning for generational wealth won't go to waste.

There's no worse situation than when everyone learns of their estate roles for the first time as the will is being read, so don't wait to discuss this subject. Take the opportunity with your children to talk through your plan and convey how you wish for everyone to work together. This simple action of transparency will be a relief to your adult children that greatly reduces stress and sets up the estate transition for success.

Get Everyone on the Same Page

The goal of the work you're doing now is to make it as painless as possible to get everyone in your family on the same page. Everyone has to agree to respect the decisions and roles for your plan to be effective.

After you've determined who is performing what role, the next step is to discuss the roles with your family and ensure that they know how to access the resources they'll need to do their jobs. You don't have to make the finances of the family business *everyone's* business, but it's important that everyone has the information they need to execute their roles.

When you have a clear plan of action and everyone knows what to do, they should also know *how* to carry out their roles. As an example, instead of saying, "When I'm gone, take care of Mom," have a plan for how that happens. What goes into caring for Mom? Who will provide care? How will it be paid for? Who is the financial advisor that can help execute this plan?

I encourage you to have these discussions in person but to also keep written documentation to act as a reminder. Consider having a written list of instructions and resources for each person to prevent confusion in the future, especially if there's a large gap of time between when you had these discussions and when the time comes for the plan to be enacted.

It might take some heavy organization, but creating a common space for information prevents your children from frantically digging through your office to find the documents they need. Thankfully, we live in a digital age and don't need boxes upon boxes of papers—but searching through thousands of computer files can be just as frustrating.

Organize your information now, and you'll save your family stress and frustration in the future.

Money Does Strange Things to Good People

All of this planning has one goal: avoid the worst-case scenarios and ensure that your gifts have their full intended impact.

Unfortunately, not everyone is a team player. Many families have someone who might not be trustworthy with money and can derail plans for generational wealth. Having clear distinctions and roles in your family can prevent unscrupulous behavior and family conflict.

Families tend to avoid tricky conversations when it comes to those in the family who are prone to mismanaging money, have a history of dishonesty, or have made bad decisions that could affect the rest of the family. Though it may be hard, it's important to be open and transparent about these concerns in your family discussions—not only because conversations behind closed doors become gossip that creates rifts in your family but also because family members who are unaware of conflicts with certain individuals can be blindsided and taken advantage of.

Furthermore, it's unfair to expect your adult children to deal with these situations on their own when they can easily be handled in beneficiary designations and instructions for inheritance in the will. You can establish a third-party trustee in your will to manage the inheritance of difficult individuals, so other family members don't bear the direct responsibility of managing them.

The truth is that money does strange things to good people and terrible things to bad people.

Sadly, even the individuals you least expect of manipulation can become manipulative in family dealings. I've seen it all. People falsely claim they're a beneficiary. Parents change estate roles on a whim or because of undue influence. Parents promise inheritances without updating wills. Secretive executors controll assets. Arguments over money tear families apart.

When you name a single executor and designate specific estate roles, it reduces the risk of such unscrupulous behavior. If you take the steps laid out in this book, when the time comes, your family's financial advisor will meet with the executor and can verify all claims to the assets to prevent someone from exerting undue influence over the finances.

When the professionals at Brennan Wealth Advisors work with executors, our role is to guide the process, be a resource for answers, and make the process easier and more understandable. We do that by discussing the stated goals of the estate owners, completing documents necessary to transition assets, and, most of all, creating a cohesive and peaceful process among family members.

Thoughtful Planning Is the Best Gift You Can Give

As the leader in your family, you bear a heavy responsibility on your shoulders. Your loved ones look to you for guidance, and while nobody has all the answers, know that you *do* have something to give: the gift of a clear plan. Your children could make assumptions or mistakes if you don't share your plan.

Maybe you've already experienced family conflict when your parents passed without a clear plan, and you had to deal with all of that responsibility in addition to your grief. Wouldn't it be wonderful to help your children avoid that same pain?

By putting in the effort now, you're sparing your children from future anxiety and conflict that will distract from your family's celebration of your life once you're gone.

One of my favorite experiences while working with wealthy families is when inheritors express how grateful they are to have had such thoughtful and caring parents—parents who prepared them for life after their parents were gone. What a gift. I hope this inspires you to give such a gift to your family.

So, where do you go from here?

Begin by recognizing what is necessary or missing from your family's wealth plan. Is it education? Experience? Is it a common approach to wealth? Maybe financial goals have not been articulated. The list could be long. Along with your spouse, your role as a leader is to share your vision, set a direction, and prepare the group to move forward.

This is your time to state what you want in both the future while you are here and the one after you are gone. You have a powerful moment in time to impact both and to teach the next generations how to handle all that will be given.

Remember, legacy is more than finances: it's passing on knowledge that each individual uses to be the best versions of themselves. Your planning provides your children with an example of how to make difficult decisions. After this planning process, your children will better understand their strengths and have an awareness of how to use those strengths to further the family legacy. And most of all, I can tell you they will be grateful.

Your family is your team, and focusing on each member's strengths is the best way to create a successful plan for your financial legacy. When you are locked in on what you can achieve together, you will achieve far more than if you acted alone.

Actionable Step: Exploring Your Family's Foundations

To get some ideas for stories worth sharing with the next generations, ask yourself these questions about your family's foundations:

- What stories of your upbringing shaped you?
- What story about your grandparents most impacted you?
- When you were young, the most important person in your life was _____ because _____.
- Are there family traditions that you carry forward that have been in your family for generations?
- In what ways do you act like your parents? In what ways do you see yourself in your kids?

Key Concepts

- Maintaining generational wealth involves family members handling many different roles.

- Choose the person in your family best qualified to carry out the terms of your will and name them as the sole executor of your estate. Appoint only one person because if you choose co-executors, you risk causing conflict and confusion within your family.

- Families that successfully manage wealth play to each family member's strengths by assigning each role to the person who will handle it best.

- Your role as the family leader is to make intentional and meaningful connections between past, present, and future generations.

- Money does strange things to good people and terrible things to bad people, so consider now who might be unable to properly handle an inheritance. Consider a third-party trustee instead of a family member to manage the inheritance of anyone prone to mismanaging money. You may need to put safeguards in place to avoid negative consequences down the road.

- Thoughtful planning is the best gift you can give your children. By putting in the effort now to plan your legacy, you're sparing your children from future anxiety and conflict.

6

Empower Your Family with a Plan

*Each generation goes further than the generation
preceding it because it stands on the
shoulders of that generation.*

—Ronald Reagan

Would you give a fifteen-year-old a car and say, "Figure it out," with no instruction, no guidance, no rules of the road, precautions, or warnings?

Of course not!

Yet, sadly, the way many parents pass on inheritances is similar to handing over the keys and saying, "Good luck."

You've done a lot of thinking about how to help your family avoid this situation. Now, it's time to act, which is why this chapter is all about getting in motion. You know the Pillars of Wealth, you've gone through some personality-identifying exercises, and you're playing to your family's strengths. Your next step is to empower your family by communicating your plan for the future—including a future when you're no longer around.

This is where Project Family Wealth starts to get a little uncomfortable. You've probably already noticed that creating generational wealth isn't a simple process. There's a reason most inheritances don't last—if it were easy, everyone would do it.

The reality is that planning your estate isn't without its challenges. You and your spouse might not be on the same page in all decisions, and there could be friction among your children. When it comes to planning for the future, the main hurdle is that no one wants to talk about, think about, or even consider their own death. But death is inevitable for us all—why wouldn't we talk about it?

As the main provider for your family, the aftermath of your death can be a major source of fear for your loved ones.

Planning for what happens after you're gone is the most important strategy you can give your family. It prevents undue turmoil and gives your family the peace of mind to step into their future without fear.

The Importance of Planning Your Will

Even though Hollywood would like us to believe that wills are a source of drama—a somber affair during which the family gathers around a mahogany table, and the estate attorney reveals your secret last wishes—the reality is that wills are tedious.

Wills require forethought, coordination, and meetings with your financial advisor and estate planner to make sure everything is in place. If not done with the closest attention to detail, your heirs could be left frustrated, disappointed, and confused.

Most of all, if the will is not coordinated with all the financial advisors (CPA, wealth advisor, and estate attorney), your estate intentions could be mismanaged. For these reasons, I take the lead for my clients, quarterbacking and coordinating these efforts among the estate professionals to make sure the investors' intentions can play out.

What most people don't realize is that many potential problems with wills can arise. People make changes to their will but fail to send the updated version to their family members or financial planners, which is the worst kind of surprise.

If your will isn't updated to reflect your most recent financial situation when you pass, promises to heirs can be left unfulfilled. If the beneficiaries in your will don't match the beneficiaries of your investments, the beneficiaries listed on your investments trump those in the will. Your intended gifts are left as just that: *intentions*.

It's a common misconception that there is a reconciliation of estate documents and accounts, but unfortunately, this isn't the case. There is no fairy-godmother estate planner who comes in and magically puts all of the pieces together after we die. Rather, it's your family that has to deal with the fallout of a messy will.

As an example, if you get divorced and accidentally leave your ex-spouse as the primary beneficiary on your biggest life insurance policy, even if your will names your current spouse as the primary beneficiary of your estate, the life insurance proceeds of the policy will go to your ex. *This is a very difficult mistake to unwind.*

Fortunately, by laying out a plan for the execution of your will now, you can prevent sticky situations in your family's future. Specificity and clarity are everything. If your will states that you want to leave $100,000 to an aunt upon your death, where will those funds come from? Is there a designated bank account? Are there investments to be liquidated? Does that amount come from the sale of the house? Without laying out the specifics, your heirs may not understand your intention.

It's essential that you regularly review and update your will so that promises don't go unfulfilled.

Let's say that you intended for the $100,000 going to your aunt to come from a savings account set aside for this purpose, but now the account totals $50,000 due to unexpected healthcare bills. The will was never updated to reflect this change. In this case, the executor must come up with $50,000 from other estate assets that may require liquidating investments. What if those investments are providing monthly income for the surviving spouse? *Now, we've got a problem.*

In general, it's important not to make promises about money that you might not be able to keep. In other words, don't count your chickens before they hatch. Life is what happens while you're making other plans, and we're in an age where healthcare expenses are rising. Life expectancy has dramatically increased, which means long-term care costs might be considerably more expensive than you planned. You might use more of your retirement nest egg than you anticipated.

Simply put, you don't know what you don't know, which is why consulting your financial advisor when it comes to the tricky aspects of inheritance can help you avoid miscommunications. So many misunderstandings occur in families over how assets will be transferred and inherited, what's taxable and what's not, what does and doesn't pass outside of probate, and whether verbal inheritance promises will be fulfilled.

The reality is that no matter what you promise your family or write in your will if that amount doesn't exist, then your heirs don't get it.

To prevent your will from having provisions that can't be fulfilled, I recommend that you review it every year with your spouse and financial advisor. Have your estate-planning attorney review your will every five years.

Your will should be shared with your financial planner, so they can work out how to generate the intended inheritance amounts while still providing for the surviving spouse. Good advisors ask good questions, so make sure to vet the estate plan with your financial advisor.

How to Use Your Estate Plan with Your Financial Plan

Once you build a plan that reflects your family's circumstances and goals, you'll review the progress toward goals each time you meet with your financial planner. Keep in mind that the plan isn't set in stone; our lives change. We reach and exceed goals. Sometimes, we miss our goals and have to stretch out the timelines. Whatever happens, your plan will reflect the changes and help you communicate that information to your family.

The Estate Plan is a key document that you'll take to your family meetings to discuss with your kids. It should be accompanied by exhibits that pictorially show the plan for estate assets, usually created by the attorney or your financial advisor. If you don't want to get into how much is in each account, you can eliminate specific numbers and show the general plan for income and expenses. It's important to avoid making promises you can't keep. For that reason, it's best not to give specific dollar amounts because you never know how much money you'll use later in life. The purpose of the plan is to convey the overall objectives without getting buried in the details of accounts, investments, and numbers that can distract from the big-picture focus.

Even though you're the driving force behind your plans, I don't recommend trying to develop a financial strategy on your own. Behind the summary and overview that the plan provides, there should be underlying calculations, projections, and an experienced vision for how the plan is going to be executed. A knowledgeable finance professional can ensure your goals are actionable and, most importantly, achievable. Your wealth advisor will be able to walk you through each step of the plan and help you realign your priorities as needed.

Communicating Your Plan to Your Family

At this stage of Project Family Wealth, it's time to plan family meetings. This is the last step of planning where you're deciding what information you're going to share with your family.

For now, the most important point to keep in mind about your will is this: the first time your family sees your will shouldn't be after your death.

If you don't discuss the will with family while you're still with them, the provisions, content, decisions, flow of assets, and expectations you've set will likely be overwhelming, especially for the executor of the will. Simply telling your children that you've made a plan isn't enough to give them peace of mind. Yet, parents typically tell their children that they have a plan in place without explaining exactly what the plan is to the very people who will carry out that plan.

The complexities of planning and executing your will are all the more reason to have consistent meetings with your family. It's not necessary that you meet every month, but meeting at least once a year ensures that everyone's questions are answered and that your plan can adapt to fit your current situation.

During these meetings, it's helpful to bring in the estate planner so they can go over the will and provisions. Also, invite the financial planner to answer questions about how the assets will flow, what's taxable, and how funds will be inherited. Encourage storytelling and discussions about family values as a reminder of the motivations behind the assets and to prevent the ugly monster of greed from rearing its head.

Adult heirs have concerns, but many of them are hesitant to ask their questions for fear of overstepping. Sometimes, they don't ask questions because they're afraid they'll create tension between their parents or siblings. It may be that the parents are standoffish about questions because they themselves don't fully understand exactly what they've put in place.

Understanding the heart of your *why* and the Pillars of Wealth will build a strong foundation for how to explain your decisions.

When you express the heart of the *why* behind your plan to care for your spouse and for the distribution of inheritances, heirs will fully understand your decisions and be prepared for their role. Communicating the *why* also insulates against any misunderstandings or hurt feelings. For example, if you explain that you've included your aunt as a beneficiary because she made significant contributions to your life, your children won't be blindsided.

Actionable Step: Organize the Keys to Your Accounts

A valuable step you can take today is to organize your passwords into a convenient map for your executor. After all, the more we move into a digital world, the more critical passwords are going to be for your family.

When you're planning your family meetings, it's important that you have an updated record of all online financial passwords, such as those for online banking, investment accounts, and credit cards. Just make sure that you're not storing sensitive information (like saving passwords in a document on your home computer) that could be hacked or stolen online.

The worst-case scenario is that your executor can't access your accounts—or doesn't even know that some accounts exist. When financial accounts are inactive for a period of time, they are rolled into a state lost-account fund where the money can fall through the cracks and your family can't immediately access it. Your family can eventually recover these funds, but it will take them much more time and effort than if you had left them the passwords and instructions.

When I have my yearly meeting with clients, I make sure we update their password sheets in our secure, encrypted client vault. We also perform annual beneficiary checks, so

there are no surprise differences between the will and beneficiaries listed on investment accounts.

What Can Go Wrong If You Don't Share Your Plan?

Now, I'd like to tell a cautionary tale about what can happen if you don't plan for the future and communicate your
intentions to your family. It's the story of how unsuccessful
families pass assets to the next generation and the ways it can
go terribly wrong.

In unsuccessful families, there are no discussions about
investments or why they are in place, where the will is, or what
the passwords are to bank accounts, home computers, and
important online information. Couples name co-executors
if they have more than one child simply because they "don't
want to hurt someone's feelings" or "they want to treat everyone equally."

In these families, the patriarch thinks the kids will figure
out how to take care of his wife if he passes before her. She
doesn't know the plan for income once he's gone and is left
in the dark. She never asks about investments, insurance, or
long-term care, and as a result, she's unaware of what the
sources of income are, how much money they have, or if they
have debt.

Meanwhile, the adult children are concerned about
what happens financially when Dad dies, and Mom needs
long-term care. They argue about what to do with financial assets—*who will care for Mom?*—and they second-guess
each other's decisions.

These families usually fall into disarray. Not only did
the stories, values, and traditions in the Pillars of Wealth go
unshared, but the financial lessons regarding asset inheritance were also not conveyed.

Making emotional, uninformed decisions about money is ill-advised. Add in clashing family personalities and the death of a parent, and one wonders how family inheritances could be expected to last. Sadly, some inheritances become a stressful, painful, and concerning experience that drives a wedge between family members instead of being a wonderful gift that imparts a legacy.

Imagine spending your life building a financial gift to pass on to the next generation, but your legacy fractures your family. "Just figure it out" is not a plan. It fails all the attributes of what successful families do in caring for the next generation.

Fortunately, if you're reading this book, I know you don't want that for your family. The good news is that you can avoid disharmony by planning your estate and communicating your vision with your family.

How to Plan and Hold Meetings With Your Family

Once you've worked with your spouse, financial advisor, and estate planner to create your plans for the future, it's time to hold a meeting with your family to discuss the details.

These meetings can happen in whatever way possible, even if it means some family members participate through video chat. You might combine the meeting with an annual family trip, which doubles as a fun opportunity to maintain traditions.

This meeting should be held with your immediate heirs, especially the executor of your will. If there are any trusts involved, the trustees should also attend. Even though you might have listed extended family members as beneficiaries, estate-planning meetings are generally done only with your adult children, as it may not be essential for extended relatives to be involved in these discussions.

I highly recommend that family meetings be moderated by a third party, ideally your financial planner. Having a moderator ensures that the family works together as a unit, that there is a clear agenda with objectives, and that no important information is forgotten. Also, when there is an expert in the room, questions can be answered in an unbiased manner.

Don't Mention Dollar Amounts

The most important tip for family meetings is that specific dollar amounts of inheritance should not be shared with beneficiaries.

The reality is that, short of having psychic abilities, there's no way to anticipate with complete certainty how much money any one of us will have left over when we pass away. Life happens: needs change, businesses fail, properties sell, markets go up and down, and health changes. It's simply impossible to predict how it will all play out.

I've seen firsthand how money does strange things to good people, and telling your immediate heirs exactly what they'll receive can be a recipe for unrealistic expectations, hurt feelings, and forgetting the *why* behind your wealth. Focus on the *why* behind the assets rather than the monetary value of the assets themselves.

Beneficiaries should know they are listed in the will, but no one should expect to inherit a certain amount. This strategy prevents your children from making plans based on unrealistic and damaging expectations.

Fortunately, explaining the general flow of assets can be done without having any dollars attached. Sit down with your financial planner to determine what would be meaningful for your adult children to know, especially the executor, and build your plan from there. Your financial planner can create exhibits for these family meetings that don't have any dollar amounts attached to the accounts, so you can still show the flow of assets.

If you're concerned because you've already told your children that they're getting a specific amount of money, it's okay.

Your plan isn't completely ruined. In this situation, transparency is key. Approach the situation with honesty. Share with your heirs that you realize it may have been premature to discuss the financial aspect of the estate since you cannot know how much will be available for inheritance when you and your spouse are gone. You might have experienced this situation with your parents if their long-term care was more expensive than expected. Share these stories, if possible, to illustrate why you're taking a new approach.

Actionable Step: Get-Into-Motion Checklist

As you prepare for your family meetings, here are a few steps that will set the stage for success.

1. Get on the same page as your spouse about your goals, vision, and plan. This is a non-negotiable!
2. Inspire your family to become a part of Project Family Wealth. The intention is to open dialogue so you can collaborate with your family members on the direction you and your spouse have decided to pursue.
3. View your family members as important stakeholders in the future.
4. Select the best person for each role in wealth management and discuss that reasoning with the family.
5. Hold a series of family meetings. The first starts with you and your spouse sharing your *why* and the story behind the money. This is where you engage your family with the purpose of Project Family Wealth and the mission of your family working together toward long-lasting inheritances.
6. The next meeting starts with the Estate Plan review. Invite your estate planner to the meeting to explain certain provisions like advance directives, financial power of attorney (POA), trusts, and executors.
7. Have another family meeting to discuss the flow of assets. Invite your financial planner to present the layout of the plan for the assets, where income comes from, and how funds are inherited.
8. Make these meetings engaging. Listen. Ask questions.
9. Use the Pillars of Wealth to brainstorm in your family meeting what your family stands for: what values do you share, what traditions do you practice, and what stories are important to carry on?
10. Help each family member identify their own *why*.
11. Encourage financial stewardship of each individual. Help them own their wealth journey by learning from yours.

Your Plan Comes from a Place of Loving Kindness

Having a plan for the inevitable future is important, but for some, it is more immediately apparent just how valuable safeguarding a family's future can be.

I have a dear friend who has three beautiful daughters, one with special life needs. Because she cannot take care of herself independently, she requires around-the-clock care. My friend has had to consider the aftermath of her own death earlier than most because she and her husband have to plan how to provide for their daughter.

I am continuously amazed at the loving kindness that provides a governing focus for her decisions. Her search for confidence in her family's security and future is rooted in how much she loves and cares for all of her children.

From my friend's loving-kindness, something miraculous happened. Without being able to speak, the daughter brought the family together. The whole family committed to their plans for how they would arrange to care for this special young woman. Everybody knows the plan, supports it, and understands how to execute it. There is no worry to hold them back from fully experiencing their lives.

In the spectrum of life, everyone will at some point need special care, whether from illness, accident, or aging. We are all going to need to have our hands held and to have someone make decisions for us.

As a reminder of all that goes into your legacy—not just the assets but the stories, traditions, values, charity, and more—the Pillars of Wealth help you make sure that

When your family is unified through your legacy of wealth and loving-kindness, every generation can confidently enter the future free of fear and able to put their best selves forward.

loving-kindness governs all of your decisions as you plan for the future. I've laid out guidelines in this chapter, but you know your family best, and your plan can be anything you want it to be.

Your family is unique, and your vision for the future and plan for passing on long-lasting inheritances should be made just for them.

Actionable Step: Imagining the Future

As you plan for the future, whether it's tomorrow or years from today, complete the following sentence to describe your vision for what's to come.

What are you here for? To . . .

- change the history of your family
- impact lives
- re-script your life and the lives of your sons and daughters
- instill confidence in those who look up to you
- be your best hero
- break the harness on your power
- start something
- finish something
- grow something
- _____
- _____

Key Concepts

- Many people assume their will, insurance policies, and other documents will be reconciled after their death, but that simply isn't the case. Therefore, it's important to keep these documents organized and aligned with your intentions to avoid potential problems, such as an ex-spouse unintentionally receiving your life insurance benefits.

- To ensure your will stays up to date, review it with your spouse and financial advisor at least once a year. Have your estate-planning attorney review your will every five years.

- Come up with a plan to discuss your will with your family, ideally with your estate planner in attendance. The first time your family sees your will shouldn't be after your death.

- Having a moderator attend family meetings ensures that the family works together as a unit, that there is a clear agenda with objectives, and that no important information is forgotten.

- As a best practice, keep an organized and up-to-date record of your accounts and passwords. Make it easy for your family to access this information if needed.

- When discussing your will with your beneficiaries, it's best not to share specific dollar amounts of inheritances. Sharing specific amounts can create unrealistic expectations and other negative reactions. Remember: money does strange things to good people.

7

Bringing the Family Together

I challenge you to make your life a masterpiece.
I challenge you to join the ranks of those people who
live what they teach, who walk their talk.

—Tony Robbins

What if your family is meant for more, and you could make it happen?

When I think about families working together, I envision a cruise ship where the captain's main goal is smooth sailing for all passengers. Among factors like a well-charted course to follow, a destination, stellar nautical instruments, and calm seas, one of the most important tools is the ship's anchor.

The anchor keeps the ship from drifting off-course, and because these anchors typically weigh 10 to 20 tons, a massive chain made of links weighing 140 pounds each keeps the boat connected to the anchor. The job of anchor management falls under the direction of the captain and plays a critical role in keeping the ship on course.

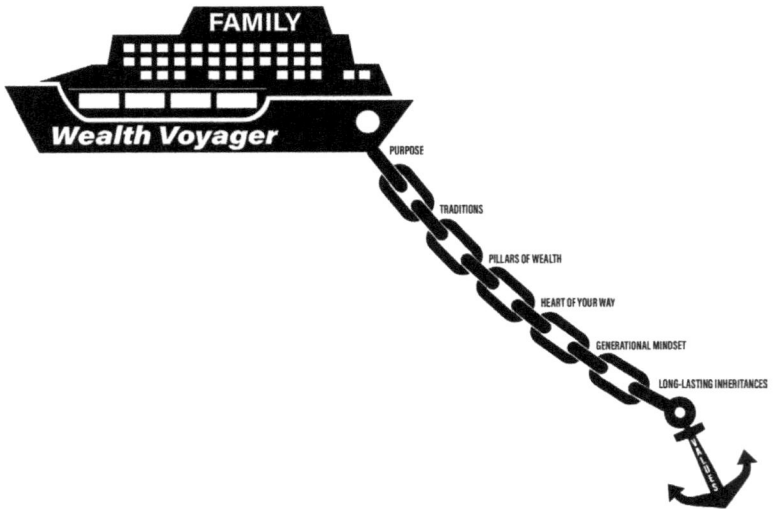

FAMILY

Wealth Voyager

PURPOSE

TRADITIONS

PILLARS OF WEALTH

HEART OF YOUR WAY

GENERATIONAL MINDSET

LONG-LASTING INHERITANCES

In your family, you are the captain planning for your family's smooth sailing in life. All the concepts in this book serve as important links in the chain, keeping you and your family purposefully connected to each other and the anchor. Together, you are strong and anchored, and you can avoid drifting off course.

Remember, you have a beautiful moment in time to impact the trajectory of your family's life.

This chapter is all about how to discuss what's often left unsaid, misunderstood, or concerning to family members. It's also about creating a way for you to discuss the Pillars of

Wealth to expand your family's wealth concepts and to give you a way to discuss Mindset, Habits, and the Future (covered in Chapter Eight) with your loved ones.

The fact that you're reading this book means you care about your loved ones' future. You want what's best for them, and you can be their hero by starting a new tradition of purposefully gathering everyone to have discussions centered on the concepts in this book, beginning with your *why*. Many families hold annual family meetings to cover a variety of topics, including financial goals, learning new financial concepts, and understanding the plan for the future. These meetings typically are also attended by the financial advisor and estate planner, who discuss the estate details, answer questions, and create an environment for all to learn. (See a sample agenda in Appendix A at the end of the book.)

In some families, when family meetings are scheduled, it usually means bad news is around the corner. This is why I encourage investors to create a tradition of openness within their families by naming the meeting.

For example, you may name your family meeting "The Smith Family Gathering," "Smith Family Bootcamp," or "Legacy Matters." Call it whatever works for your family. This makes meetings more light-hearted and promotes a feeling of togetherness.

By naming the practice and integrating it into your family life, it becomes easier to create space for these conversations.

The First Conversation Happens with Your Spouse

The first conversation to have is with the person closest to you in Project Family Wealth: your spouse.

Your spouse might be receptive to this perspective on wealth...and if she is, kudos to you both! In my experience, however, some spouses may not feel comfortable being involved. If that's been your experience, I have some tools in this chapter to help you engage your spouse.

Engaging others is all about the approach talk.

It may be more effective to engage her from the Financial EQ perspective instead of the Financial IQ—the emotional *why* perspective, not the practical *how* perspective.

Let your spouse know you're worried because she is not involved, and you want her to be prepared in case something happens to you. She needs to hear this. Conversations like this are more loving for your spouse and your entire family. They are at the heart of making long-lasting inheritances.

Years ago, I had married clients who were both high-level executives in the telecom industry. I met with the husband only. His goal was to formulate a plan for him and his wife to retire in ten years. We developed a plan with specified projections that included how much they should invest monthly to meet their retirement income goal, how to pay down debt, and what type of long-term care insurance could be considered. He and I met year after year to make sure the plan was on target. I had several phone conversations with his wife, but work responsibilities kept her from coming into the office.

Finally, the time came for them to retire, and I met Sarah. The meeting began with details about how and when income started and from which investments it would be distributed. I discovered early in my career that people learn best pictorially, so I provided a timeline for their retirement on a single piece of paper.

When Sarah looked at their timeline, she said, "Oh, thank goodness, we won't run out of money!"

I could see the relief on her face, and she began to cry. For ten years, Sarah had been terrified that she and her husband would run out of money in retirement like her parents did because she wasn't engaged in their financial plan. Her lack of participation wasn't due to a lack of financial knowledge, planning, or ability to keep projects on target. She had invested a significant amount of money over her lifetime, was successful in her career, and managed hundreds of millions of dollars in budget money for her company.

Even so, she didn't wade into these financial conversations because it was such a close topic to her that she was hesitant to get involved. All this time, we didn't realize she carried a silent fear of running out of money in retirement.

When you have these conversations with your spouse early on, they won't carry the burden of silent worry about the future.

Sharing Your Plan for the Future

Without a target, you'll miss it every time. In family wealth, that means you need a plan for your family to unite for inheritances to last. Connecting heirs to *why* you've invested, saved, and planned for the future is the critical first step with family.

Your plan will determine how your family addresses health issues, who will be in charge of financial decisions, and how inheritances will be distributed and controlled. Most importantly, as you're forming a plan, think about what you want in the future. What vision do you have for your family? How can this project enable everyone to live incredible lives of financial independence and purpose?

You may consider having one-on-one conversations with each family member so you have a sense of what concerns are best to discuss in your group meeting.

It's important to communicate your wishes to your heirs as you approach retirement, otherwise, you leave your future care up to your children's discretion.

One of our clients ran his own business, and his wife participated administratively in the business part-time but wasn't fully involved. When he was suddenly incapacitated, the business struggled. His wife didn't understand how to run any of the systems to keep operations going, and she wasn't privy to the company's finances. This resulted in much fear about her future and, ultimately, the business closing. If, instead, the couple had attended financial meetings together and had a continuity plan for the business, the company would likely have been able to continue operations.

We never expect an accident, divorce, or business failure, but by sharing your plans with your family, you can ensure that everything won't come crashing down at the first sign of trouble. This is most important for business owners to realize. Business continuity plans are crucial for small business owners. Being the only one with the keys to the kingdom puts the business and your family at risk.

Lay the Foundation for Successful Conversations

Sharing your plan for the future is only part of the conversation. Another goal of these discussions is to address your family's concerns and questions. Concerns about money affect us all, and this worry often keeps important financial conversations from happening. Individuals worry about money. Families worry about money. We worry about each other.

How can we address concerns and uncertainty about our financial futures?

Actionable Step: The "I'm Worried about . . ." List

This exercise should be one of the first activities you do together with your spouse as you plan for difficult conversations about wealth. Perhaps your spouse has worries you're not aware of that should be addressed in your planning—this exercise will help bring them to light.

To complete the activity, you and your spouse should answer the following questions individually. After creating your lists, share them with each other and see if you're on the same page.

- What are you worried about with regard to your spouse?
- What worries do you have about beneficiaries?
- Do you own a business? How will that be passed on?

- How will you care for your parents?
- What concerns do you have about retirement?
- What expectations do you have about financial decision-making?

The beauty of this exercise is that it puts everything out in the open. I recommend first completing it with your spouse and then with the other members of your close family.

As the one who handles finances for your family, it's natural for you to engage your spouse first so you both can lead the way through these conversations. Creating space for open conversations and making it acceptable for your family to share their concerns is a monumental first step that can be relieving for everyone.

Removing the mystery of family money is often not practiced or even thought about, but it ought to be. Success in this endeavor comes down to communication, connection, and transparency.

Transparency is the most effective way to dispel self-limiting storytelling and eliminate concerns. Right now, you may not have thought about explaining the financial decisions you've made or what happens when you're gone. You might assume that if you were to die today that your family would figure it out, but they don't have the same information, experience, or familiarity with finances as you. That's why it's so valuable to get them involved now by being transparent and starting these conversations.

This isn't to say that you should pull out your bank statements and share your entire financial situation with your children. When it comes to transparency, what matters is that you share the *why* behind your decisions, such as whom you're naming as the executor of your will and what role everyone plays in the execution of your estate. This is how you get your children involved in these big conversations about family wealth. Your adult children simply want to know there *is* a plan and what is expected of them.

To create this openness within your family, encourage transparency and lead by example. You may consider starting with a simple question to your spouse or adult child, such as, "Do you have any worries about our retirement or what to do when I am gone?"

Other questions to contemplate would be:

- Who would you call first about finances if something happened to me?
- Do you know how to access my computer, our bank accounts, and our investments?
- Do you know where our insurance policies and estate documents are?
- Would you be interested in hearing (or working on) the plan for when I am gone?

Having money should not bring with it concern and confusion. You've worked all your life with a plan in mind for a long, happy retirement spent with family, travel, hobbies, charitable endeavors, and giving your time and talent to enrich others. If that plan dies with you, what have you really left your spouse and inheritors?

How to Address Family Concerns

If conversations about plans for the future are met with concern from your spouse, sharing your worries is one way to start the conversation in the right direction. Try approaching it this way:

You say, "When you _____, I
_____."

For example, "When you avoid talking about money, I worry about your future when I am not here."

You would have your wife's attention for sure if you were to say, "The reason I'm interested in our finances, estate planning, and insurance is that I love you, and I want you to be taken care of for the rest of your life. You are the heart of my *why*, and so are the kids, and I would like you to understand what to do when I'm not here so that I know you'll be okay."

This is an important role in which your spouse can be active. She relates to Financial EQ, and this can be a real motivator in bringing the rest of the family along. She can speak to why this is so important to you both, why these conversations are necessary, and how broadly wealth can be defined.

Imagine the peace of mind your family will experience. Also know that from my vast interactions with inheritors, your gifts of time with them, family traditions, and your thoughtful planning for the future are what they cherish. They'll also learn a valuable lesson from you on how to organize their own financial house and prepare for the future.

Financial health and planning always seem like major obstacles, but they become a normal part of life when done a little bit at a time. Think of this step as simply having a conversation with the people you love. Put that way, it doesn't sound complicated at all.

Bring the Conversation Back to What's Important

Many families struggle to talk about wealth, but successful families move past their issues by keeping conversations focused. If your discussions about wealth get sidetracked, remember what's most important—the principles and values that define your family culture:

- Leadership
- Unity
- Culture
- Respect
- Communication

Family culture creates a connection to the estate you've built and ensures that your gifts will endure.

Everyone wants to leave their kids meaningful and long-lasting inheritances, but without a strong family culture, inheritances and family members may go their separate ways. There's no togetherness created. No respect for wealth that is inherited, no stories passed on, no heart of the *why*, and no understanding of why Mom and Dad worked so hard. Everything in Project Family Wealth is geared toward connecting the next generation to the *why* of their inheritance.

So many discussions, research studies, and white papers focus on culture in corporate America, but we rarely consider creating a purposeful family culture. When we talk about hiring and team building, it all comes down to the right culture fit. But we don't choose our families; it takes intentionality to create a culture in your family of togetherness, traditions, and family stories.

Practice Micro-step Planning

How do you eat an elephant? One bite at a time.

As I'm sure you've realized by now, family financial planning is a huge project, but it can be broken down into more manageable micro-steps. The whole process starts with simply having a conversation with your spouse. Another micro-step is to contact your financial advisor so they can deal with complex, behind-the-scenes finance calculations that serve as the foundation for your plans.

Get in motion and reduce big goals to sizable, workable, and achievable steps. Micro-steps are tasks achievable in twenty-four hours. They are anything you can do in the next twenty-four hours to get in motion. What can you do tomorrow to get started? Even better, what can you do today to set you up for the next step tomorrow? Continue to focus on micro-steps each day as you move toward your milestones.

Only progress matters—where you stand this year compared to where you stood the year before.

The Greatest Gift Is Caring

To make Project Family Wealth a reality, it's going to take you being all in for your family. When we hear the phrase "all in," we usually think of incredible Olympic athletes who have dedicated their lives to training, and all of their intentions are focused on that single sport. It's not easy. When you're having conversations with your family, you're doing the hardest part. But if you only do it halfway, your hopes for long-lasting inheritances may not be realized.

How are you passing the culture of stewardship and responsibility to your children to build in their own families? What narratives are you conveying to your family?

In my family, the story of my grandmother's immigration to America from Ireland is a cornerstone of our identity and approach to life. It drives the heart of our *why*, and for good reason: stories drive connection, and connection drives long-lasting inheritances that go beyond financial gifts.

Without communicating your *why*, your legacy may not have meaning, and your children might forget the family's history and be frivolous with the hard-earned assets they've inherited. We tell stories about great families because we want to lead meaningful lives and be remembered. If you go all in, your family's legacy can outlast you.

Key Concepts

- Concerns about money affect us all, and it's this worry that often keeps important financial conversations from happening.

- Follow best practices for effective conversations:
    - Be open.
    - Get to the heart of the matter.
    - Include your *why*.
    - Start now.
    - Schedule time.
    - Use strategies.
    - Work with financial professionals.

- In the conversations you'll be having around wealth, an important goal is to have a united front with your spouse and convey the importance of your life goals.

- Transparency is the most effective way to dispel self-limiting storytelling and eliminate concern.

8

The Rules of Wealth Wellness

I think purpose is one of those things that brings you that sense of well-being.

—Ben Nemtin

At some point in life, everyone thinks about winning the lottery and never having to work another day in their life. But what if I told you that most lottery winners go broke?

An amazing story from Michelle Crouch in *Reader's Digest* tells a stark story about lottery winners: "Life after winning the lottery may not stay glamorous forever. Whether they win $500 million or $1 million, about 70 percent of lotto winners lose or spend all that money in five years or less."[4]

---

[4]   Michelle Crouch, "13 Things Lotto Winners Won't Tell You: Life after Winning the Lottery," Reader's Digest, March 15, 2024, https://www.rd.com/list/13-things-lottery-winners/.

Hard to believe, but true.

What separates people who win big and then lose it all from those who work hard and create wealth that lasts across generations?

Success comes down to three areas that play important roles in our ability to accumulate and transfer wealth: mindset, habits, and outlook on the future.

What I know from my experience with investors is that the older we get, the more of ourselves we want to leave behind. It's why grandparents sit next to grandkids at family gatherings and why we share stories of our lives with our children. We want to connect the next generation with who we are, how we got here, and what shaped us. Who wouldn't want to leave more of themselves behind, especially if it means helping those we care about live their lives to the fullest?

When we do this intentionally, it gives meaning to the financial inheritance that is also left behind—it gives money purpose. The story of your life—your *why*—inspires the next generation and creates the foundation for the successful passing of long-lasting inheritances.

The purpose of this chapter is to help you launch discussions with your family using the coaching techniques I've shared with investors. These topics can jump-start conversations with your family as you begin to hold regular family get-togethers around wealth and help you guide your family in the lifelong pursuit of wealth wellness.

This is also a great chapter to share with the young people in your life. Strengthening the foundation for financial wellness at a young age shapes people into good stewards.

Taking Responsibility for the Financial Future

Successful families have figured out that the three areas of mindset, habits, and future outlook hold the key to long-lasting wealth wellness. These categories may sound simple enough; however, life is full of distractions that can pull us away from our financial priorities.

What will you do to safeguard yourself from distractions that take you away from your wealth goals?

Each of us is responsible for our financial journey, whether we're female or male, married or single, young or seasoned, where we've come from, or what we've experienced. With this mindset, avoiding distractions can be easy, but we must keep this mindset in focus.

You, and you alone, have the ability to create the life you want for yourself and your family. Thank you, America!

Plant the Seed Today

I've witnessed how the application of these rules has created an immense generational impact out of consistent financial investments over a lifetime.

Don and Betty were some of my first clients in the early nineties. During those same years, one of my favorite career memories is hosting a financial radio show with my dad every Saturday, educating investors in the Dallas-Fort Worth area. Don and Betty faithfully listened to our show and did everything we asked our listeners to consider. Their goals were to have enough money to retire comfortably while also creating an inheritance for their two kids. They were committed to making monthly investments, and in this way, they grew their wealth.

Now, their two adult children have become clients of mine, and they have hundreds of thousands of dollars that they inherited due to their parents' habits and consistency. They're now putting this money into investments to pass on to their own children.

Even now, when Don and Betty are gone, their money is still here and will continue to grow because they've instilled the proper habits and mindset in their heirs. In turn, those habits will be passed on to the next generation. What a legacy born out of dedication. I'm often amazed when I reflect on the lives I've crossed paths with in business and the amplifying effect good money habits have on families.

Prioritizing sound money habits is what it takes to have a happy life, retire well, and create a long-lasting inheritance.

Don and Betty proved that. Through their consistent monthly investments, they made a significant difference in the lives of their adult children because of their wealth management early in life. They didn't make huge financial sacrifices but were dedicated and faithful investors.

The Rules of Wealth Wellness

As you prepare to have discussions about wealth with your family, I encourage you to use this list of topics to spark conversation.

Creating a mindset for habits to become real leads to a bigger future.

Mindset → Habits → Bigger Future → Long-Lasting Inheritances

MINDSET

Even though habits are arguably the most important component of lifelong wealth wellness, mindset comes first. If you don't have a healthy mindset that allows you to commit wholeheartedly, it's hard to believe habits could be sustainable.

1. Be present.

Viewing the past as instructive is how successful people turn personal history into life lessons. You are not who your parents or grandparents were, and you're not who you used to be, either. All that matters is for the past to become instructional.

Good money habits can be established anytime in life, which is why being present and forging your own path is an immensely important lesson to learn as well as teach your heirs. As a Strategic Coach® member for decades, one of the biggest lessons I learned is *being present enables gratitude.* That's so powerful to realize and pass along to your family.

2. Live in gratitude.

Gratitude is a virtue. From what I've observed between family members, the families who practice gratitude have amazing connections with each other. This promotes a sense of togetherness, support, and thankfulness for everything in one's life. When we let more gratitude in, it allows less space for attitudes of jealousy, comparison, and unnecessary competitiveness. Gratitude is the gold standard for families that wish to connect heirs to meaningful inheritances.

3. Believe you are worthy.

There are people who believe that someone else should govern their money and plan their future. Many women who support their families by working in the home believe they should not be involved in big financial decisions. Young people tend to think investing is not what they should do at their age, and they miss out on the great opportunity of time in the market. Others think that only rich people invest, so they hesitate to begin investing.

Money wellness is a symptom of our thoughts. It takes one decision to start a lifetime of habits that achieve financial strength. Do you have someone in your life who planted the seed for you to begin your path to financial independence? Could you be that someone for your family? Investing and having money is for everyone, but it starts with a healthy mindset of believing that this is true.

Everyone is capable of becoming a successful investor.

4. Know that you are in control . . . of *everything*.

There are times when a life situation seems to be beyond our control, but being passive is no solution. There is always something to do or a lesson to extract. Allow yourself to believe that you have control over your thoughts, actions, and reactions in every situation. This mindset can have a powerful effect on wealth aspirations. Money insecurity is simply a symptom of having a scarcity mindset.

Believing you and your family can have financial security is a necessary mindset to achieving that security. When you accept that you have the power to change your life, you'll be able to take the first steps to get there.

5. Think BIG.

Thoughts shape our reality. An effective way to change the course of life is to think bigger than your current situation. Someone thought to build the first suspension bridge, create the first computer, eat an octopus, go to the moon, inject penicillin, build an electric car, create cloud computing, get out of a bad neighborhood, and create a life different from how they were raised.

Thinking big when it comes to your financial future is just like all the other ways we think big and dream about our lives. Everyone can think big. There are no restrictions on our thoughts and starting good money habits.

We seek counsel from our parents or our mentors when we're applying for jobs, taking a promotion that requires more from us than we thought we could offer, or starting a new business that has never existed before. The confidence you can offer your children is part of what you have to give. Another layer of wealth. To help your kids and grandchildren think big, be mindful of how you can offer encouragement and support.

6. Money is a mindset.

Being relentless in the pursuit of protecting our mindset by not thinking "if only" thoughts is a trait of successful families. "If only I could….If only we had….If only that didn't happen" are dangerous thoughts to entertain.

Consider Nick Vujicic, an Australian man who was born with no arms or legs. At the young age of ten, he attempted to take his own life because he couldn't see a reason to live. Thankfully, he survived, and today, he's married, a father to four children, an athlete who enjoys fishing and golfing, and a massively successful motivational speaker who has shared his message of hope around the world to seventy-four countries.

Nick's joyful life is in defiance of the "if only" mindset. He found a way to live his life without limits, and because Nick has a mindset that anything is possible, he made it a reality.

Maintaining a positive mindset is a skill under constant construction. Life brings regular challenges, but what matters most is how we react to them. Approaching life with resiliency is the best way to protect our mindset.

7. Money prefers no gender.

To this day, harmful stereotypes persist and disempower women from taking control of their financial situations. When women internalize stereotypes, they hold insecurities and beliefs about their capabilities. For this reason, many women don't want to be involved in financial affairs because they don't believe they have the skill set to be active participants.

In my experience, most husbands want their wives to be involved. Even though many women trust their husbands to wisely manage their finances, their disinterest can create hidden strain. Her husband worries about what she and the family will do once he's gone, and she worries about the same thing.

One of the best life lessons you can instill in your teenage children, especially your daughters, is that they have a responsibility to invest in themselves. Talk to them about their future selves. Help paint a picture of what it might look like when they buy their first house, start a family, launch their career, or start their own business. Let them know that whatever they dream is within their reach.

Give them the power to impact their future now before insecurities and gender stereotypes have a chance to create barriers to success. Confidence is a tremendous gift.

HABITS

Once you've established a healthy mindset around wealth, you're ready to start forming good money habits that will last a lifetime. Habits play a critical role in the legacy we ultimately leave behind.

8. Build habits that empower you to direct your own financial fate.

Life might have been different if any one of us were born into an extraordinarily wealthy family, but that shouldn't stop us from creating wealth. If you believe that your situation is out of your control, financial success becomes unattainable.

It's easy to assume people who are financially successful have always been successful. The truth likely involves a huge amount of hard work, risk-taking, and sacrifice behind the scenes—years of wise investing, budgeting, and smart habits—that brought the person to where they are today.

If you take control of your own financial fate, you can experience success by committing to good habits today that accumulate over time.

9. Invest now.

A highly effective habit of successful investors is that they start saving early and invest regularly. Smart investors know that it's *time in the market* and not *timing the market* that matters.

No matter your age, it's never too late or too early to start investing. When people ask me when they should start investing, the answer is always *right now*. Think of the saying, "The best time to plant a tree is twenty years ago. The next best time is today."

The same is true in investing. If you wait a month, a year, or five years, you will have missed out on everything you could have gained from being in the market right now.

Time in the market is what builds wealth. It's dangerous to think there's time to invest later. Investing later requires a bigger financial outlay to meet goals, and it's hard to know how much time each of us actually has. Trust me, your future self will appreciate your dedication to investing early in life.

Introduce your children to investing early as well, even if they are only contributing $25 to $100 per month. When your children learn discipline in investing early, they build the habit and dedication that will help them throughout the rest of their lives. One day, they'll set a good example for their own children, and the discipline you started will echo through generations.

10. Focus on longevity, *not* a retirement date.

In the same way the checklist of estate planning is an outdated tool, so too is the old tool of targeting a specific date for retirement. So many people think of their retirement as a date circled on the calendar rather than a well-planned vision for the decades that follow it. With just a date in mind, investors often don't think about setting accumulation targets for retirement. Too frequently, the day someone chooses for retirement comes and goes. They wake up the next morning and ask, "Now, what?"

Have you ever thought about the prospect of being unemployed for twenty to thirty years? I like for investors to retire *to* something, not *from* something. If only the retirement date is the goal, investors can miss the more important habits for retirement: setting retirement goals around retirement income, determining how to pay off debt, and most importantly, creating a plan to have the retirement of a lifetime. If you want to travel and take your grandchildren on trips, where will that money come from? How will you pay for long-term healthcare and have the ability to pass on money?

Longevity is all about answering these questions. Do the work now to secure financial stability in the future and be able to actually make your vision of the future a reality.

11. Use SMART financial goals: Specific, Measurable, Achievable, Relevant, and Time-bound.

SMART goals are not "I want to send my kids to college, buy a vacation property, or retire early." Those objectives are too vague; there's no way to objectively know if you're on target or missing it. If your goal is to buy a lakehouse that is valued between $500,000 to $1,000,000 within five years, those parameters will help you make a specific plan and know if you're on track.

It will be easier to plan for specific goals now rather than wait until these decisions are knocking at your door. Creating time-bound goals allows you to capture relevancy. In other words, if you don't have a time factor associated with your goals, there's no way to make projections. When clients determine their window for retirement, we'll often run multiple projections so they can see what difference one, two, or three years make in retirement income.

12. Review your estate with your spouse.

Review investments and insurance annually with your spouse so you both understand where your money is allocated and who is listed as the primary and secondary beneficiaries wherever you name beneficiaries (will, retirement plans, life insurance, annuities, etc.).

Do this with your financial advisor to make sure the beneficiaries listed on your investments are consistent with your plan.

Hopefully, your spouse is involved in all financial decisions, but if not, it's important to bring you both closer together in this effort. This should be non-negotiable. It's essential that your spouse knows where family money is, how much there is, and what the plan is for income once you're gone. Speak from the heart and let her know that you're worried she may not be prepared for when she will have to make financial decisions.

These simple efforts create peace of mind for family members and minimize confusion and fear-based decision-making.

FUTURE

Inheritances are all about planning for the next generation, which is why—like much of the material in this book—the Rules of Wealth Wellness require you to look toward the future.

13. Know the difference between savings and investing.

Saving is a tool for short-term goals, and investing is for the future. Savings are for unexpected expenditures and short-term goals in the next twenty-four months.

For long-term goals, investing is better suited. Whether you invest in real estate, stocks, bonds, mutual funds, ETFs, your 401(k), or IRAs, investing is about using the tools you have right now to build wealth in the future that supports your ambitions.

When you invest, you're allocating money for five to twenty-five years down the road. Time in the market allows money to compound. Think back to Chapter Four when we talked about using the Rule of 72 (see page XX) to calculate how many years it will take your money to double. Assume a savings account pays 1 percent… that will take you seventy-two years to double your money.

14. Your spouse's goals should not be yours.

Your goals are just that: yours. It's best to plan for each spouse's life goals that complement the other's. Being married does not mean your personal goals and investment styles are married as well. You and your spouse are separate people who complement each other, and your investing styles should do the same. Here are a few reasons why:

- Spouses likely are not the same age.
- One may be conservative with investments and the other more aggressive.
- Life expectancies are different for women and men.

I recommend that both spouses have money in their name and have their own stated goals that support the overall objectives they share, such as when they plan on retiring.

15. Pass on a legacy of smart money habits to your family and friends.

If you are the first person in your family to live on a budget, own a savings account, free yourself from debt, build a seven-figure investment account, or graduate from college, share the wisdom and encourage those you care about. Don't keep your knowledge to yourself!

Some people hoard information because they think they're running a financial competition, but the truth is that comparison is not how to achieve goals. If you use your knowledge to lift up your colleagues, friends, and family, they'll do the same for you. Shared knowledge is powerful. Many of my most successful clients purposefully have conversations with their friends about money, which is usually considered a taboo subject but shouldn't be. These clients don't talk about how much money they have, but they are open about what they're doing in the markets, and they share smart tips freely.

Usually, whenever someone is the first person in a group to do something, it's because there was someone in their life to move them forward, share knowledge, or give them a leg up. Sharing your wisdom with those you care about is a meaningful way to invest in the future. Never assume that someone probably has everything already figured out because there's always guidance to offer and receive.

16. You are what you think.

You are what you think, which is why successful people tend to carry empowering thoughts about both their money situation and the future. They know maintaining a positive outlook directly impacts their ability to achieve goals. Meanwhile, negative talk and thoughts keep us in the past and debilitate forward progress.

As I reflect on my most successful clients, they would never tell you that they came from the school of hard knocks, even though they share stories about their upbringing and how tough it was for their family to financially make ends meet. Rather, they use hard times and even failures as lessons instead of letting their past weigh down their future.

If we keep thinking that the sky is falling, it's going to change who we are and how we respond to the world and our families. If we expect the worst, what lessons are we giving to our families?

Thinking positively opens doors of possibility and opportunity.

17. Retire to something and for something.

Most retirees I work with enjoy retirement because they planned a life of exploration, enjoyment, and, yes, working. They cultivated what I call a "retirement side hustle," where their passion or hobby becomes the area of focus in retirement, whether it's travel, time with grandchildren, volunteering, or even working in their dream career. Doing more with your time and freedom defines modern retirement.

With decades at their disposal, there is every reason today's retirees can and should work where, when, and if they want. Working keeps the mind and body engaged and maintains a vital social spark. Retirement also creates space for the fun activities you've always wanted to do but didn't have time for while you were making a living.

You don't have to be any less active in retirement. You can, in fact, be free to engage more with life.

Start Creating Your Legacy Now

In my years of financial advising, during which I've worked with thousands of families, I can say with confidence that successful families consistently follow a shared set of practices: they commit to prudent money habits, lead by example, keep a healthy mindset, openly communicate, believe each person has a unique perspective, and value individual strengths.

In short, successful families follow the Rules of Wealth Wellness—and this can be your family's recipe for financial resilience, generational wealth, and legacy-building.

Wealth wellness is immensely important to your heirs, and it isn't just about personal success—it's about leading your family to be good stewards of all the wealth aspects in their lives. Start having these conversations now and use these rules as a framework during your family gatherings to ensure that you pass on the right tools for your legacy to last.

Key Concepts

- Success in family wealth comes down to three areas that form the Rules of Wealth Wellness. These rules play important roles in your ability to accumulate and transfer wealth: your mindset, your habits, and your outlook for the future.

- Families that successfully manage wealth grow their net worth through consistency: investing monthly, not racking up debt, and creating good money habits.

- Having a healthy mindset around wealth is key to growing your net worth and creating habits that stick.

- Once you've established a healthy mindset around wealth, you're able to form good money habits that will last a lifetime.

- Plan for the future by investing long-term, avoiding debt, setting goals, and passing on good money habits to your heirs.

9

Make Your Words Last for Generations

To love ourselves and support each other in the process of becoming real is perhaps the greatest single act of daring greatly.

—Brené Brown

Many investors worry their children or grandchildren may squander an inheritance, be poor stewards, or neglect the lasting impact they've been gifted.

My clients talk about how they were frugal during their lives and made sacrifices for their families. They'll say, "Even though I love cars, I didn't get a sports car because I was investing that money in my child's future. I don't want them to get their inheritance, blow it all, and neglect to give their children the same opportunities I gave them."

This chapter is about how you address this fear. Of course, there are times when inheritors are connected to values, stories, and the emotional quotient of inheritance and still blow money. However, by connecting your children with these intangible aspects of wealth, you're improving your odds of long-lasting inheritances.

To aid you in starting the conversations we covered in Chapter Seven or to convey messages that are easier written than said, start by writing letters to your family. These letters allow you to acknowledge and celebrate each member's unique contributions and explain your reasons for the life you built.

Letter writing can be a powerful tool for expressing what was important to you when you were growing your family, why you made certain career choices, why you saved and invested, and what you hope for the future.

See where the heart of your *why* shines through and use that *why* to ground your conversations with your family. When you welcome your family a little bit more into your heart, they can understand what was important to you, what is important now, and what you want to be important in the future.

So why do some inheritors squander money?

Maybe it's because they didn't know what to do with the money. Maybe it's because they never connected to the reasons you accumulated your money or estate. Or, maybe it's because they were kept in the dark and ended up surprised by their inheritance. No matter the situation, do you really want your hard-earned money and the sacrifices you and your spouse made to go into the hands of inexperienced inheritors—inheritors who are not educated on what you want them to do and the right way to do it?

Maybe we don't all have stories of a grandmother who immigrated from Ireland or someone who started a family business, but a common story many can relate to is that their parents were frugal because they were thinking about you and the family you were going to start, and they wanted you to have an inheritance that would make a difference in your life.

Don't miss writing your own story. You might not think it's important, but it connects your inheritors to the *why* behind your accumulation. My grandmother, who was truly poor when she came to America, would think we were all crazy for sharing her story because she never thought there was anything important about what she did at eighteen. We, on the other hand, found great meaning and inspiration in her story and courage. Unfortunately, she didn't talk about it often. Yet, her story still became a meaningful part of my life, and it has connected me to the importance of managing my estate along with my husband and telling her story to our sons. So, keep in mind that your stories may not seem significant to you, but they could be powerful to your family.

You can't control how your kids act, but you can influence them by sharing your values.

One way to do this is by writing letters that your family will cherish. Writing letters to your family is an important and ongoing step in the process of creating generational wealth and financial resilience.

Seize This Moment and Put It in Writing

It might be morbid, but death never goes the way we expect it to. Often, we have a romanticized idea of dying in someone's arms and having the perfect moment to say things to our loved ones about our lives together. Many times, this just isn't the case.

Letters are a way to say what might be left unsaid. Right now—this very moment—is the richest time in our lives. We have our health and the people we love around us. After all, you're reading this book because you care about your loved ones' futures.

Seize this moment because once it's gone, you'll never have it again. Only a minute ago, I was a minute younger. And an hour ago? You guessed it: an hour younger. Now, go back a year, ten years, twenty.

No one needs to be reminded how quickly time flies because even looking at your children or in the mirror is a reminder. No person on Earth will ever be able to reclaim the time that has passed, so take life's opportunity in front of you and tell the people you love the most how you feel about them.

I have been witness to this very practice from the beneficiaries' perspective when a parent dies. The admiration, respect, and deep love that a letter from a parent can conjure are quite breathtaking. Add to that a well-intentioned distribution of estate assets, and it becomes something heirs tell stories of as well as organize themselves to do the same for their heirs. Do not underestimate the power you have in written words.

You can tell your family you love them all the time, but sometimes people need to hear a little more than that. Even if you only write one letter, it will be cherished for the rest of your family's life. **But let's not wait until a diagnosis because these letters aren't deathbed letters.** They're about seeing the importance of this moment in time and making important things *important* by doing them now. Intentional, personal letters that your family members will cherish say a lot more than the mechanical "See you later, I love you!" that we voice every day.

I watched how gut-wrenchingly sad it was for my mom to not have the ability to say goodbye to my dad. I also witness my clients have this experience because, inevitably, we have clients who die every year and have to enact their last wishes with their families. We've learned through talking to the surviving spouse and inheritors that the aftermath of death is unexpected, no matter how many preparations are made.

With that in mind and already understanding the importance of estate planning, let's not make death this cold, legal business at the end of a life. Let's make estate planning an inspirational, loving connection because that's the core of long-lasting inheritances. I cherish the letters I've received from my parents during my lifetime. If I don't inherit a single dime, I'll have inherited a lifetime of inspiration and character qualities that can't be quantified.

Intentional communication and connection change the relationship between parents and children for the better, and it reinforces your legacy as a family. If a family only talks about making money and transferring it upon death, then that's the extent of their legacy, and the parents' hopes and dreams for their inheritors seldom are realized because they were divorced from the family's core values. Letters are the vehicle that will pull the heart of your *why* into the estate-planning process.

Forging Family Bonds

Before you give letter writing a second thought, you should know that letter writing is a tradition with an impressive history. It's also a way for you to be all-in for your family. President George H.W. Bush was a prolific letter writer, and before modern communication, letter writing was not only essential but considered an art form. Thomas Jefferson, George Washington, and Abraham Lincoln all wrote incredible letters to their friends and families.

Also, contrary to what might be expected, this intentional form of communication is especially important in today's digital world. Despite the ease of communication, we just aren't that connected.

I'm incredibly fortunate that my parents have always been letter writers. My parents wrote letters to my siblings and me, and before they had kids, they wrote letters to each other, which we had the privilege of reading later in life.

When my dad passed in 2017, my mom needed help going through his belongings. One day in my dad's office, I opened a drawer in his desk and found a stack of mementos. There were papers, cards, pictures, notes, and letters. I even found a copy of the letter he had written me after my graduation from junior high. I've always cherished this letter from him talking about how impressed he was with all I'd done at a young age and what I meant to my parents. I was the first-born child in my family after my parents experienced miscarriages, and they've never failed to express this history to me and the meaning behind it, which was only able to become a part of my identity because they took the time to tell me. I inherited my desire to make important things *important* from my parents.

The night before my wedding, I stayed at my parents' house. I spent that night writing them a handwritten letter. Before we left for the church on the day of my wedding, I propped the letters on their pillows for them to read when they came home from the wedding reception. It was the perfect opportunity to express my appreciation for them.

They taught me the importance of thoughtfulness, and I've carried on that value in my own life. I thanked them for everything they had done for me, for giving me the ability to not see limitations, to be confident in everything I do, and for teaching me how to be a responsible leader.

These letters can be life-changing to write and for your children and grandchildren to read, and I wouldn't want these letters to go unwritten because they can be so pivotal in your life now.

Sometimes, it's hard to say the things you want to say in person, which is why letters are invaluable, especially if you have trouble expressing thoughts and emotions face-to-face.

When I found the letter I wrote the night before my wedding in my dad's desk drawer, I cried all over again like I did when I wrote it. I can't even imagine if the only way I could have communicated that was to verbally say it to my parents. Letters give us time to contemplate what's important and to memorialize that time. My parents also wrote letters to my husband and me when our sons were born, and they wrote letters to our sons on their birthdays and graduations.

None of these letters had anything to do with finances or an estate, but they had everything to do with passing on values, love, encouragement, and inspiration. When I'm going through a rough time, these letters are a way to pick myself up, dust off, and get back in the saddle. Even though my dad is gone, I can still find comfort in his words.

Meaningful communication can come in so many different forms. Maybe you're not used to writing, but your wife is. Recognize her unique strengths and work together, especially if you've never done this before or are unsure about the reactions you'll receive. I hope my personal stories express the value of starting this tradition from your children's perspective. When you share heartfelt thoughts in letter form, your children will cherish them for the rest of their lives.

Bring Unity to Your Family with an Ethical Will

Letter writing has a storied past among former presidents and other influential leaders in history, but it also has a place in today's estate-planning process.

Consider ethical wills, which are non-binding documents derived from the Jewish faith. This tradition began centuries ago but continues to this day, and these letters describe ethical values to be passed on to the next generation. If you've never heard of ethical wills despite their history, it's likely because they're not included on most estate-planning checklists.

Ethical wills typically explain why certain decisions are made in your legal estate-planning documents. Ethical wills don't require a financial professional or an attorney to create. You can write them once in your life or multiple times to individual members or the family as a whole.

The ethical will is an important supplement to the two kinds of legal wills that are included in estate planning documents: the living will and the last will and testament.

A living will is a document detailing a person's wishes for medical treatment when they are not able to give or convey consent. A last will and testament directs your intentions for the distribution of assets and care for minor children. The purpose of the ethical will is to describe your *why*, impart the estate plan, pass on values, express your hopes and dreams for your family, or address special care or considerations for a family member.

Use a letter as the space to recognize each family member's uniqueness and how they contribute meaningfully to the family. These letters also serve as an impactful way to pass down family stories and ensure that they won't be forgotten. For example, you may choose to use a letter to give a glimpse into your life and the obstacles you've overcome, and it can be the way you encourage your family to do the same.

Ethical wills work best when they include gratitude, inspiration, encouragement, life advice, and an expression of love.

This is the time to convey to your spouse and heirs why you've made the decisions you've made. Why is this person the executor? Why did you start your business? What do you wish for in life for your children? What are the family qualities that you want to continue on and embellish for decades to come? And, certainly, include your vision for their future.

Remember, when it comes to estates, surprises hurt people. Many wealthy families leave a large percentage of their wealth to charity after their death. From their children's perspective, however, they wouldn't want to grow up seeing an accumulation of wealth and then discover once both parents are gone that all of it is going to philanthropy.

An ethical will gives you the opportunity to explain why certain beneficiaries and charities were chosen and to inform your children of the estate plan well before it's enacted.

Best Practices for Impactful Letter Writing

Are you ready to put pen to paper? I'm sure you already have some ideas of what you'd like to include in your letters. Know this: these letters can be about anything, for anything, written at any time, and as long or short as you wish. I've included these best practices for letter writing to help you in the process. You can also read a couple of wonderfully written example letters in Appendix B.

Always Date Your Letters

There isn't a card I write that isn't dated. Why? Firstly, because letters contain your thoughts from a particular moment in time. The context of that time is important to the letter's message.

Secondly, you give someone a letter with the hope that the person is going to keep it. I know that I treasure everything I receive, and your children will treasure your letters, too. When they look back at your writing one day in the distant future, they'll want to know exactly when you wrote it.

Give Letters for Meaningful Events

When it comes to letters, timing when you give them is important. The next time you put estate documents in place or need to amend them, take the opportunity to write a letter. The letters can be given at the time of the estate planning meeting or at a family meeting. If you do set a family meeting for a year from now, that's going to give you a lot of time to think through the exercises in this chapter and start writing letters individually or to the family.

You can also write letters annually and on special birthdays, life events, occasions, and graduations. Each opportunity you take to write a letter is another brick in the wall of the legacy you're leaving behind. Even if you write a letter to a spouse or a child, your descendants generations from now can look to that letter as an example of the values they've received that came from your lifetime.

Start Writing Now

If you're overwhelmed thinking about how many opportunities there are for letters, try micro-stepping. Let this chapter be a place where you can immediately begin to take notes and get into motion. Jot down a few points you want to make, set aside just five minutes to brainstorm, or start this tradition by writing a small note to your spouse.

Most importantly, if you don't schedule time for these letters, they won't happen. What's the next important date that might warrant a letter? When do you want to give the first letter? Put these dates on your calendar. You'll be glad you did.

The best first audience is your spouse. You can wait for her birthday or an anniversary, or you can write a letter just to surprise her. The good thing about letters is that it's the practice itself and the thought behind it that matters. Your writing doesn't have to be worthy of a museum archive to be meaningful, and if you're worried about your handwriting, a typed letter is better than none at all.

Use Letter Prompts

Prompts can be an effective way to get the letter-writing process started. Try starting your writing with one or more of the following and see where it goes:

- It's important for you to know...
- I'm not so good at saying certain things, but I've always thought you are incredible because...
- You have added so much to our family by being...
- When I think about your future, it makes me smile to know...
- Life can be challenging at times, which is why I want you to know...
- I like to imagine that when I'm gone...
- When you were born, my love for your (mom or dad) and our family grew because I knew...
- I know this for sure...
- What will always be true is my _____ for you.
- One of the most important lessons I learned when growing up is...
- My favorite memory of you is...
- When I think about what you will inherit, I hope it includes much more than financial assets, like...
- Above all else, I want you to know... (you may include your *why* here).

By following these best practices, you'll keep your letters focused, compassionate, honest, and true to the heart of your *why*—everything necessary to get through to your loved ones and bring them on board with your vision for your family.

Family Meetings Aren't a Substitute for Letters

Writing letters allows you to reach your family in multiple ways, and while there might be some overlap between your letters and family conversations, family meetings aren't a substitute for the letters.

Conversations about your estate and letters to your family complement each other. These letters aren't deathbed messages to be opened after you're gone, but a tradition to uphold for the rest of your life. Similarly, an ethical will provides family-unifying moments to encourage your family while you're alive and to get them connected to the reason you're building your estate.

Estate planning is simple until it isn't. You can try to control as much as possible through actions like setting up trusts for specific ages. But if your family isn't truly and deeply connected to your intentions and the heart of your *why*, the most detailed planning may not have the impact you hope it will.

Estate planning can get complicated, which is why it's more important than anything that your inheritors are connected to the heart of the *why* behind your money.

I suggest using writing as an opportunity to get your thoughts down instead of replacing discussions with letters. Then, use your notes to help guide you through a discussion without relying solely on them. After a particular hardship has passed, a letter is the perfect opportunity to express everything left unsaid about the situation, including how proud you are that your child navigated their way through a stressful situation.

It's All About Your *Why*

With a letter, you're solidifying the story behind wealth—the heart of your *why*. You're creating a legacy while you're here, but your heirs will take it and own it for decades to come. They amplify your legacy: the person you were, the values you instilled, the examples you set, and the community impact you had. Each generation can be better than the one that came before it, but it takes intention and effort on your part to guide your family's values.

Everything we've done in this book ties back to one purpose: to connect your family to who you are and why you live the way you do. Money is simply a tool to influence your family for the better, to give them beautiful lives and to express your love for them. You are the heart of your family, and when you connect your influence to something tangible—letters, inheritance, assets, traditions—your legacy and your family's will endure and amplify over the generations.

Actionable Step: Brainstorming Questions

Here are some questions to get the inspiration flowing as you contemplate what you want your letter to be about.

- What non-financial inheritance gifts do I hope will enrich my family?
- What stories and lessons are especially important for my family to know?
- How can I encourage each family member to dream big?
- How can I recognize the uniqueness of each family member?
- When I think about my children's future, what do I see and hope for them?
- What helped me during tough times that could help my family too?
- What seeds do I wish to plant in their minds for the future?
- Is there wisdom or life advice I have to share?
- What values are important to our family?
- What experience in my life taught me a lesson that is still with me today?

Key Concepts

- Letter writing can be a powerful tool for expressing what's important to you. Why did you make certain career choices? Why did you save and invest? What do you hope for your children's futures?

- Letters are the vehicle that will pull the heart of your *why* into the estate-planning process.

- Letters can be life-changing to write and for your children and grandchildren to read; they will likely hold on to them for the rest of their lives.

- Also, consider writing an ethical will. Ethical wills typically explain why certain decisions are made in your legal estate-planning documents.

- Follow letter-writing best practices: always date your letters, choose the right focus, give letters for meaningful events, start writing now, and use letter prompts.

Conclusion

You Have a Powerful Moment in Time

I hope this book has illustrated family success is not just about financial knowledge and assets.

As for my family, my dad may be gone, but his legacy still lives on through us. The heart of my *why*, which in large part came from both my parents, influences everything I do. With the legacy my father created, I see the impact of his tenacity and courage in my life. My husband and I strive to embody the family values we inherited from our parents in our own family. That's the power of a generational mindset.

> You have a powerful moment in time to impact your legacy and the legacy of your family. Your role as a provider is about so much more than wealth accumulation. It's about passing down values and connecting with family.

Now that you're at the end of the book, I hope you think about wealth in a completely different way. Maybe this book surprised you because you expected rows of numbers, investment portfolio advice, and in-depth market discussions. Wealth isn't just stocks, bonds, investments, and assets. We've expanded wealth to include what's truly important: family culture, values, stories, and generational connection. Imagine what your family could accomplish not just today but in one hundred years if you and your heirs truly internalized these concepts.

You know your family best, which means you can apply the content in this book at your discretion. But my suggestion is to try something new. Even if your family doesn't have a tradition of talking about money or family culture, it's never too late to start. You might be surprised at your family's willingness to try these concepts.

As the provider, you've been faithful to your family's needs. You've done an excellent job. Look at everything you've accomplished for your family and all of the opportunities you've given them. I know it has taken hard work—sacrifice, investing, saving, building a career and a home, and managing the financial decisions for your family. You've done well on the financial side of the ledger. Now that you've created security for your family in the present moment, don't miss the opportunity to provide in a different intangible and everlasting way.

Take just five minutes and brainstorm all that you have to give. Shift your thinking from the 401(k), lakehouse, and investments. Instead, consider these: life experiences, advice, time, wisdom, support, and encouragement. What's in your wealth treasure trove? What can your family treasure? What can make a difference in their life that is beyond estate assets?

You've done great so far, and now you can do even better by taking the concepts in this book and using them with your family to create a legacy that encompasses inheritance in all of its forms. As the Open Ensō you've seen throughout this book represents, life is a journey, and I hope you continue to enjoy yours while building strong connections within your family.

The Steps of Project Family Wealth

Be assured that you've already done the hardest part—accumulating wealth, providing for your family, and making financial decisions for your household. Just as you've taken the steps to get to where you are now, maybe with a few stumbles or setbacks, it's time to push forward with making Project Family Wealth a reality for your family.

Wealth isn't necessarily a linear process. Neither is unifying your family and connecting them to the *why* behind your estate. Even so, there are core steps in the process of creating generational wealth and securing peace of mind for your family.

Let's recap the steps to make Project Family Wealth a success:

1. Discover the heart of your *why* to understand the motivations behind your financial goals. The importance of your *why* can't be overstated because this is what will drive your financial planning and what will inspire your family to continue your legacy and responsibly manage long-lasting inheritances.
2. A generational mindset is about creating a multiplier effect for your family. Ask yourself, "What could my family achieve across generations?" When

you're intentional with your wealth and what values you pass on to your children, you create a family that moves together financially.

3. To establish a generational mindset in your family, understand the difference between Financial IQ and Financial EQ, the how and why of wealth, and collaborate with your spouse.

4. Use the Pillars of Wealth (experience, assets, legacy learning, and purpose) to compartmentalize the legacy gifts that are created over a lifetime. Without these pillars, families don't leave purposeful legacies.

5. Think of your family as a team moving toward the same goal of generational wealth. Each generation creates a stepping stone that builds on top of the others. Recognize the unique strengths of each family member to bring out your family's full potential and set the stage for generational wealth. Most importantly, get everyone on the same page.

6. As the provider, your death is a source of fear and worry for your family. Use the pillars to empower your family to create an active and purposeful connection between the estate plan and the next generation. Planning for what happens after your death, and thereby eliminating unnecessary worry, is the most important gift you can give your family.

7. Every family has uncomfortable topics that can remain unmentioned—subjects like illness and death. If these topics remain unaddressed for too long, they can weigh your family down from reaching your full potential. It's important to not avoid the tough conversations and instead learn how to address these topics with your family so your plan for your family—or your family itself—doesn't fall

apart after you're gone. Use the heart of your *why* to engage your family in these discussions.

8. Building wealth is one thing, but keeping it is another. To become a successful generational family, use the Rules of Wealth Wellness to build, maintain, and intentionally pass on wealth in order to create a family legacy.

9. Life is short, and often, it's shorter than we expect. Take the time now to write letters to your family that express everything you'd rather not leave unsaid. Creating an ethical will also helps connect your family to the values you want to impart and explains the decisions you've made. When your family is unified, they're able to create long-lasting wealth and family values that ripple throughout the generations yet to come.

Start with the end in mind. You've learned these concepts and have a format. Now, set aside time to make your vision a reality. If you've taken the steps in this book, they'll culminate in connecting with your family throughout your lifetime and beyond.

Finally, if you do one thing, let it be writing a letter to your family. It requires only introspection, and no concepts have to come forward except for the heart of your *why*. The heart of your *why* is the core of Project Family Wealth, and without it, the rest of these concepts won't come together.

A Parting Letter to You

In the previous chapter, I encouraged you to write letters to your family, and in the spirit of leading by example, I'd like to part ways with a letter from me to you.

I believe in divine intervention. Over the course of my life, I've viewed every time that someone has entered my life as intentional. It's intentional that you have this book—my book—and now we've met each other, in a way. Now, I'm going to share with you my vision for the future you can create for yourself and for your family once you put this book down.

I hope that wealth in your family becomes redefined in such a way that it furthers the family connection. You have a strong family bond, memorable traditions, and meaningful conversations. Through these actions, everyone in your family naturally takes care of each other and has the courage to address tough conversations that bring your family even closer together. Your spouse engages in family financial discussions, and your adult children have a deep connection to each other, family values, and your unique family culture.

My vision for you and your family is that you have peace of mind about your finances. Everybody at some point in their life has worried about money, but these worries don't plague your family anymore. You're not worried about your wife because she's come into the fold. Your children understand your decisions and trust that Mom will be well cared for in her twilight years. You're not worried your children will inherit assets and squander them. You had a family meeting with your advisor, and now everyone knows the plan and is connected to the heart of your *why*.

Peace might be the best inheritance of all. It's why so many families have turned to me to guide them through their finance management: my job is to be a peacemaker for families with money.

Peace of mind is the endgame for Project Family Wealth. It's my endgame in every interaction I have with investors. Peace of mind is what I wish for you—the freedom to tackle the rest of your life with confidence and love to spare.

Find the Right Partners for Your Financial Journey

I talked about successful families throughout the book, but I don't mean only successful financially. The point is that you don't have to live in a mansion to be successful because success is so much more than lasting financial inheritances. Wealth is the foundation of your family legacy, and it's your job to build off of that foundation to create the values that ensure your wealth feeds a bigger picture.

For Project Family Wealth to be a success, your financial team is as important as the team of your family. A positive outcome results from both teams working together. Very few financially successful families think, "Maybe I can do this on my own and save some money."

Having a lifelong relationship with a Financial Advisor can reap exponential benefits in the future, especially when it comes to the value of eliminating worry in your family. Successful families recognize the need for professional relationships.

My wish for you is that your financial advisor prompts these conversations, encourages family meetings, and is a source of confidence. If you're not getting what you've read in this book from your financial team, it's time to find an experienced team to provide a path forward for your family's legacy. You'll find financial firms across the country, including mine, with professionals who genuinely care about helping you create your family's future.

It's a noble career to be a financial advisor. I've dedicated my entire career to helping families think about wealth in a broader context because I've experienced the value first-hand. The sheer joy of guiding a family through their wealth struggles is why I founded Brennan Wealth Advisors. I like to say that while we handle investment planning, insurance, and retirement planning, we also handle the other side of money. I love nothing more than to watch families flourish and come into their full potential.

I have no doubt that your family will thrive as well, now and for years upon years to come.

Wishing you the best in health and wealth,

Michelle

Appendix A

Legacy Matters Agenda

This sample agenda shows common discussion topics for a family meeting as well as the person (or people) typically responsible for each.

- Mom and Dad:
    - Introductions – Family and Professionals
    - What is our *why*?
- Estate Attorney:
    - Estate Plan Concepts
    - Executor and Trustee Roles
- Financial Advisor:
    - Exhibits – Financial Plan for Retirement
- All:
    - Q & A

Appendix B

The following sample letters, excerpted from author Anthony Segil's poignant book *Love Notes: Letters from Parents to Children*, can serve as inspiration when you sit down to write your own letters.

Your Baba Will Always Be Here For You

Written by Bob Kaufman

Dear Kaz, Noah, Mica,

A Few Words From Baba. I love you.

I love you so much that the simple action of writing this letter seems like an insurmountable task to fit into words, what words alone simply cannot convey.

I look at each of you with pride, admiration, and sheer amazement. You are all unique and wonderful and totally full of life, curiosity, and intelligence.

Kaz: You are a mensch. Warm, caring, mature, talented, fun and you have an emotional intelligence seldom seen in this world. You are genuine and extremely considerate to all. You also have a talent in elevating the spirits of those around you. As an athlete, you are a specimen. You have incredible raw talent, great intelligence, and instincts, and that coupled with your ability to be the ultimate teammate will take you far. I love you, I admire you, and I totally trust your way. You make me so proud with everything that you do, and I am with you every step of the way.

Noah: You are truly one of a kind. Your intelligence, eye for detail, and complete understanding of all that happens around you, and all that happens around everyone, allows you to have a perspective unique and more comprehensive than all others. You also are decisive and have a keen ability to hone in on exactly what you want to accomplish, and once that happens, there is no stopping you. You also have a big heart and are full of passion. Please be cognizant and considerate of others on your journey to accomplishing the great things that I know that you will accomplish. I truly get you, I love you, I admire you, and I am always there for you.

Mica: My beautiful little girl. I love your ability to command every situation. You have stood your own ground with your brothers and have developed into a beautiful person—caring, brave, loving, happy, and strong. You are the torchbearer of happy, and as such you lighten up everywhere you go. You possess great leadership tendencies, and your caring nature for others will guide you to do great things and help others. You make me smile every day, and I love you more than I could possibly convey. Your Baba will always be here for you.

Kaz, Noah, Mica, the true hero of the family is your mother— Ka-san. She is my best friend and the CEO of the family. She is our pillar of strength and the best partner I could ever have on a journey through life. We have been together now for 18 years, and I love her more every day. We have a beautiful family and the best kids in the world, and together we are a solid family unit. This is because of your mother. Thank you, Naomi, for your patience with me, your dedication to the family, and your leadership as the CEO of the house. I love you.

Love,

Your dad, Bob (A.K.A. Baba)

Boys and Girls: Be Confident

Written by DJ Melzer

Dear Huntley and Jack,

We love you both more than anything in this world, and you taught us a love we didn't know until we met the two of you. Momma and Dadda have a few words for you.

Love each other and love others. Family is everything, so take care of them, love them, and respect them. Love yourselves the way we love you, and never tolerate disrespect, especially from yourself. Be kind to others, even those who don't deserve it, because it's a reflection of you. Surround yourselves with others who are kind and happy because life is too short for anything else. Life will be full of choices, and if you don't like the results, make new choices because it's never too late. Home is not where we live, it's who we are, and you will always be loved and welcome at home.

Jack: Be confident. Be kind to girls, and NEVER break up with a girl over the phone. Shower every day with soap and cut your nails. Always put the toilet seat down. Learn how to do your laundry and always eat breakfast.

Huntley: Be confident. Never lose yourself, and be true to your dreams. Don't chase something that is running (i.e., men). Learn to stay organized and NEVER gossip. Take care of your hair and skin, and love yourself. Learn how to drive a stick shift, and don't be afraid to get dirty.

Lastly, patience, kindness, trust, love, self-respect, respect for life, faithfulness, forgiveness, and peace never steered anyone wrong. Remember these words and live by them in life as you live your lives to the fullest. You deserve that!

Loving you every moment of every day,

Mommy and Dad

About the Author

Michelle Brennan Hall is a veteran wealth advisor with more than thirty years of experience guiding investors' net worth and financial decisions. Known for creating the Financial Life Map Strategy™ which fosters investor financial strength and well-being, Michelle understands the importance of clarity about the road ahead.

Michelle is passionate about giving to others through local community involvement. Serving alongside her sons at local charities and supporting many national causes with her husband is an annual family commitment.

Connect with Michelle at BrennanWealthAdvisors.com

THIS BOOK IS PROTECTED INTELLECTUAL PROPERTY

EASY IP™

The author of this book values Intellectual Property. The book you just read is protected by Easy IP™, a proprietary process, which integrates blockchain technology giving Intellectual Property "Global Protection." By creating a "Time-Stamped" smart contract that can never be tampered with or changed, we establish "First Use" that tracks back to the author.

Easy IP™ functions much like a Pre-Patent™ since it provides an immutable "First Use" of the Intellectual Property. This is achieved through our proprietary process of leveraging blockchain technology and smart contracts. As a result, proving "First Use" is simple through a global and verifiable smart contract. By protecting intellectual property with blockchain technology and smart contracts, we establish a "First to File" event.

Powered By Easy IP™

LEARN MORE AT EASYIP.TODAY